"This is an excellent book for leaders who want an all-in-one resource for building high-impact ministry teams. With terrific breadth and a focus on the big picture, *Leading from the Sandbox* will prove an invaluable resource for pastors and ministry leaders who want to move their teams forward."

— SHANNON BARNES, senior advisor, The EDGE Consulting Group;
president, Imagen Consulting

"T. J. Addington presents a clear and practical blueprint of organizational and leadership excellence. His high-impact best practices are powerful tools for purposefully advancing the kingdom of God."

— STANN LEFF, executive director of organizational leadership and
administration, Calvary Memorial Church, Oak Park, Illinois

"T. J. Addington understands the fundamentals of teamwork and boardsmanship. His principles will provide unity and alignment to all church leaders who desire to be a high-impact team. This book is a must-read for all my staff and elders."

— GLEN MARTIN, senior pastor, Journey of Faith Church,
Manhattan Beach, California

"I've been an avid student of leadership and its impact on organizations for three decades. *Leading from the Sandbox* sheds profound yet simple clarity on the subject. A must-read for any serious student."

— DONALD HAAN, CEO, Knight Transfer Inc.

"Every time I direct a staff meeting, engage in strategic planning, evaluate a staff person, plan a ministry event, or direct a volunteer, I find the word *sandbox* flowing from my lips and drawing my mind back to the principles and leadership wisdom found in this book."

— VINCE MILLER, staff director, Twin Cities InterVarsity Christian Fellowship

"This book is crucial for those wanting to discover not only the value that clarity will bring to their ministry, team, or organization but also how to achieve that clarity. The sandbox graphic alone is more than worth the price of the book. Enjoy!"

— BOB ROWLEY, Texas–Oklahoma district superintendent, EFCA;
adjunct professor, Dallas Theological Seminary

"With a new executive pastor starting soon, I couldn't have asked for a better road map to guide our first weeks together. This book will reorient and break many a leadership team free from well-worn ruts of inept team activity, advancing them to intentional kingdom gain."

— BRAD BRINSON, senior pastor, Two Rivers Church, Knoxville, Tennessee

"*Leading from the Sandbox* gave our leadership a common vocabulary for sifting through years of programs and slogans to clarify why we exist and what we want to accomplish. Think of it as both a seminar and an on-site consultant."

— DAVID HEGG, senior pastor, Grace Baptist Church,
Santa Clarita, California

"The creative and practical paradigm of the sandbox brought clarity to me and our church leaders. I am a better pastor and leader because of the wisdom in this book. "

— MARK BRUNOTT, pastor, First Evangelical Free Church, Lincoln, Nebraska

"We have adopted every aspect of this book and are experiencing the benefits of a healthy ministry. I fully recommend *Leading from the Sandbox* to any organization wanting to develop, empower, and release healthy teams into a very broken world."

— KURT DILLINGER, president/founder, Life International

"T. J. Addington is known around the world as a high-impact leader. Read this book and you'll not only thirst to be part of a high-impact team, you'll be better equipped to lead one."

— LEARY GATES, founder, BoldPath Life Strategies

"Of the many books on leadership that I've read, *Leading from the Sandbox* is the reference I consult most often. It lays out concrete principles, illustrations, and tools that both seasoned and young leaders will find transferable to their ministry setting."

— SCOTT OWSLEY, senior associate pastor of adult ministries,
Hillside Evangelical Free Church, San Jose, California

"T. J. Addington has put on paper what every thoughtful and growing organization needs to put in place to be all God intended. Read this book and see if it helps you become the leader God wants you to be. You will not be disappointed."

— DR. ROB HARRELL, senior pastor, First Evangelical Free Church,
Austin, Texas; board of directors, EFCA

"*Leading from the Sandbox* is written by a proven leader who lives and breathes the same principles every day in his organization and personal ministry. Don't miss the impact this book offers!"

— MARK BANKORD, founder and directional leader,
Heartland Community Church, Rockford, Illinois

This book is dedicated to
Grant and Carol
and
Ken and Barb
with appreciation for
many years of friendship.
One could not have
better fellow pilgrims
or greater friends.
Thank you.

To my prayer team,
who sustained our family
through some dark days.

And to each member
of ReachGlobal
and
national partners
who faithfully serve
across our world
building His church.
You are a joy to serve.

CONTENTS

ACKNOWLEDGMENTS

What I have learned about healthy and high-impact teams has come from a combination of my own mistakes, observing great teams (and some pretty bad ones), consulting with many leadership teams in churches and Christian organizations, and learning from others who did it right.

I want to thank Bill Hamel for the opportunity to serve on a great team along with Jot Turner, Steve Hudson, Alvin Sanders, and Fritz Dale of the senior team of the Evangelical Free Church of America (EFCA). I owe a great debt of gratitude to each one who serves with me on the senior team of ReachGlobal (the international mission of the EFCA that I lead). They are a dream team and I am blessed to have each of them. And to Lindsay, who is one of the greatest team members one could have and whose support made it possible for me to write this book in the midst of a busy schedule.

My teammate Steve Hudson is the guru of intentional living. He has influenced much of what I know and practice in this arena. He taught our organization the concepts of Key Result Areas, Annual Ministry Plans, personal retreat days, and annual planning retreats. In these areas I stand on his shoulders and am better for it.

For ten years, Grant and Carol have given our family a place to relax in the mountains of Montana. It was there that a substantial part of this book was written. Thank you, friends.

T. J. Addington

HOW TO READ AND USE THIS BOOK

There are several ways you can read and use this book.

You can read sequentially from chapter one through chapter nine.

Or, if your organization already has a clearly defined and functioning (1) mission statement, (2) set of guiding principles, (3) central ministry focus, and (4) culture (all of which are necessary for high-impact teams), you can start with chapters one and two and then jump to chapters five through nine, which focus on building and leading healthy teams.

If you have specific needs you want to explore, each chapter opens with the "CliffsNotes" of that chapter, so you can get a feel for its content.

If you peruse the book, read the title pages and pay attention to the shaded statements, which highlight key principles. In addition, stop and read the pieces labeled, "H. I. Best Practice," "H. I. Moment," "H. I. Definition," and "H. I. Questions."

Ultimately, I hope you will use this book with your ministry team so that together you can build the healthiest possible high-impact team. If you do so, the H. I. Moments and H. I. Questions at the end of each chapter will be helpful as you dialogue with your team.

If you resonate with what you read in this book, I encourage you to use it as a training module when you bring new members on to your team so that the team shares a common vocabulary and understanding. I also believe church boards will find this book helpful as they think about how they operate together or how their staff teams should work. My prior book *High-Impact Church Boards*[1] is specifically designed to help boards become healthier and more intentional, and church governance systems empowering rather than controlling.

INTRODUCTION

"What comes to mind when you think of *team*?"

When I have randomly asked that question, people's first thoughts are often pejorative. Not because they don't want to be part of a team. They do. But their experiences on a team have so often been negative, unhappy, or even brutal.

Even so, people crave the team experience. They long for a healthy team where they can "take the hill" with people who share the same missional passion. They want to work synergistically in collegial relationships under visionary, empowering leadership. Many of us would give a lot to find that kind of team.

The fact that you picked up this book indicates you know teams matter, in spite of the challenges and frustrations we face in leading and serving on them.

Having done ministry on my own, on teams that were teams in name only, on some massively dysfunctional teams, and finally on a healthy, collegial, missional, and passionate team, I will never willingly go back to doing ministry by myself—or on an unhealthy team. I love doing ministry with a healthy team of aligned and competent folks who are committed to a meaningful mission. I have the double blessing of serving on that kind of team and leading that kind of team.

This book is written out of a passion to help ministry teams in the church, in mission organizations—in all kinds of ministries—develop this kind of high-impact team for the sake of Christ's kingdom. I've written out of a passion to make our common ministries fun—a joy in the journey.

Over the past twenty-five years I have served as a pastor, as an organizational and church consultant on governance and leadership, and as an organizational leader. I have been on good teams and bad teams and been fortunate to lead some great teams. Today I lead a global organization of more than five hundred people, almost all of whom are on a team. My goal as their leader is that all of these teams would be healthy, missional, and effective. This book is written for my colleagues in ReachGlobal and for my colleagues who lead and serve on ministry teams in the church and in other ministries.

What sets this book apart from other books on teams? Very simply, it is practical and written as a "how to" manual on developing high-impact teams. This book will help you:

- Lead from personal health
- Hire healthy team members
- Deal with unhealthy team members
- Lead with maximum clarity
- Determine your central ministry focus
- Keep everyone aligned around mission
- Develop Annual Ministry Plans
- Lead with a mentor/coach mentality
- Help people undergoing leadership transitions
- Foster a culture of empowerment and accountability
- Use the sandbox as a leadership tool
- Define the culture of your organization
- Become more missional
- Focus your team on results rather than activity
- Overcome the five dysfunctions of ministry organizations
- Help people minister out of their sweet spots
- Demolish silos in your ministry

When they are done well, teams can help our ministries move to new levels of effectiveness, compared to what any of us can do by ourselves. Good teams are powerful ministry accelerators that result in missional alignment and enhanced ministry results.

I "lead from the sandbox," hence the title of this book. If you played in a sandbox as a youngster, my guess is that you have pleasant memories of it. The sandbox was a place where creativity and fun were synonymous. Likewise, I believe our ministries should be fun and challenging and use the best of the gifts and creativity God has given each of us. Leading a team is all about understanding the giftings of those we lead and then releasing them to "play" to their strengths, literally to play in their work.

The metaphor of a sandbox can become a simple tool that brings maximum clarity to your team regarding what your organization is about; it keeps your mission, guiding values, central ministry focus, and preferred culture out in front at all times. When these key elements are summed up through this picture, the "sandbox" allows leaders to empower people within clearly defined boundaries and brings alignment around ministry philosophy rather than methodology. And the picture has a high "get it" factor, which is a big plus for any of us who lead complex organizations or teams. Chapters 2, 3, and 4 will unpack how you can lead from the sandbox.

CHAPTER ONE

FALLACIES AND PRACTICES OF HIGH-IMPACT TEAMS

CHAPTER SUMMARY:

Many people have a faulty understanding of what it means to serve on a team. This includes thinking that teams are about working with our buddies, getting our emotional needs met, doing life with our close friends, spending lots of time together, attending meetings, or working on the same project. Or, that because we are a team, we lead by committee.

No! A high-impact team is a group of missionally aligned and healthy individuals working strategically together under good leadership toward common objectives, with accountability for results.

High-impact teams are different from most teams. High-impact teams are:

- All about alignment of the whole organization around a passionately held common mission
- Synergistic in harnessing the various gifts on the team and focusing on the bottom line, which is delivering on the mission (i.e., achieving results)
- Egalitarian in culture, where robust dialogue is encouraged
- Led by healthy leaders who love to empower and release team members to do their thing

- Characterized by a commitment to results, good emotional intelligence among members, and meaningful meetings

High-impact teams do not just happen. They are developed and empowered to achieve ministry results.

People hold many ideas of what *team* means.

For people who are highly relational, there is a sense that a team should be made up of "my best friends with whom I do life and who meet my emotional needs." For those who are deeply missional, team is about task and little else. Some people love spending time with their teams; others would rather get on with the pressing priorities crowding their schedules.

Differing expectations come from what we may have read about teams (much of it not very helpful), our own experience with teams (good or bad), and our personal makeup.

There is also a great deal of angst and cynicism regarding teams—both in the ministry world and the secular world. Many of us have served on teams that were highly dysfunctional, which colors our desire (or lack of it) to serve on another team. At other times, the tension comes because teams are teams in name only; if anything, they hinder rather than help our work. Sometimes team leaders are ill equipped to lead and therefore frustrate those who must show up for meetings.

I assume you are reading this book because you are not satisfied with the often ineffective, average- or low-impact teams you have observed or been a part of. Or, you want to take a good team to the next level.

While there are many different kinds of teams, the thesis of this book is that high-impact ministry teams function in a way that maximizes their missional results. High-impact teams *look* different from the average team. In this chapter, we will examine fallacies about teams and the practices of high-impact teams.

FALLACIES: WHAT TEAMS ARE NOT

Lack of clarity on the purpose, practices, and relationships of teams creates tensions, frustrations, and unmet expectations for many.

Teams are not about working with your best friends. While you may serve on a team with people you consider good friends, teams are ultimately about common mission rather than working with your best friends. Missional friendships are different from personal friendships. Missional friendships are collegial relationships focused on a common mission and organization.

This does not mean healthy teams are not friendly. Members should care deeply about one another and may even share a fair amount of their lives with each other. However, the depth of friendships on teams will vary widely since personal friendships are based on shared interests and passions, while team relationships are centered on missional alignment. When individuals see their teams as primarily about friendship, it makes it difficult for them to be honest with coworkers about issues that need to be addressed. They don't want candor to interfere with friendship.

The important issue is not to confuse the role of teammate with that of best friend. The latter is a bonus but not a given.

The primary function of teams is not to meet one's social and emotional needs. If teams are not primarily about friendship, then they also aren't about meeting our deep personal needs. The deepest of these will be fulfilled among family and friends. Some social and emotional needs may be met by those on our team, but it is not a given.

Our role on a team is a functional one designed to achieve a specific mission. Teams are not designed to meet our primary social and emotional needs, and if we try to make them do so we will be disappointed when our needs are not met or when roles change. We may or may not be with our team long-term. Our responsibilities may change. The team may change. A decade ago I hired a good friend to direct a ministry I had started. He later confided to me that when he came, he had been excited that "we would do life together." In reality, as he gave more time to the ministry, I gave less time and ultimately handed it over to him completely. While he is satisfied with his role and has built his own team, he was initially disappointed that "we" did not remain "we" as the ministry grew.

I love working with the senior EFCA team I serve on as leader of ReachGlobal, the international mission of the EFCA. We have been through incredible times together, enjoyed great highs, and endured more than a few low lows. We know each other exceedingly well, protect each other, love to be together, and are committed to one another. We have seen one another through individual challenges, have prayed for family situations, and have sharpened each other to become better people and leaders. I cannot imagine a better team. *But . . .* each of us understands we are together because of the mission we serve. We seldom socialize outside of work; we each have sets of friends who meet our personal, social, and emotional needs. We are deeply fortunate to work with people we love, respect, know, trust, and value. However, we understand that our team is not built on our emotional or social needs but on the mission we serve together. This is a critical distinction of a healthy team.

Teams do not necessarily spend huge amounts of time together. Teamwork does require time—more than some people consumed by personal priorities want to give. Yet it's often less time than some who desire comradeship would like to receive.

If you joined a team when a ministry was small, chances are you enjoyed a lot of quality time together. Pressures were not great, the staff was small, and water-cooler time was relaxed. As ministries grow, however, time becomes more precious and the time spent with your team becomes more focused and strategic. Those of you on a ministry team in a church that has transitioned from small to large know exactly what I mean. And I would guess the transition was painful because your relationships had to change as well.

Healthy, aligned, synergistic teams make adequate time to be together. But they spend that time primarily on mission and secondarily on relationships.

Teams are not primarily about meetings. One of the greatest fallacies people hold about teams is that they primarily mean "meetings." They do not. Yes, teams probably must meet on a regular basis. But the concept of team has far more to do with how we *think* about our working relationships, our alignment with others in the organization, and our common mission than it has to do with formal meetings.

The senior team of the EFCA, for instance, meets one day each month. While this meeting day is sacred and none of us would miss it, my commitment to that team influences every other day of my month. As a team member, I am obligated not to cause problems for others in the organization—which means I must be aware of consequences to other departments when I make a decision. Service on the team means I must think beyond the part I oversee to consider the whole. What I do affects others! My commitment to align with the rest of the organization informs whatever I do as the leader of ReachGlobal. I have no option to play the lone ranger or to lead my ministry in a vacuum.

A team mind-set always takes into account the whole organization: its best interests, its success, and the interrelated ministries team members may represent. This is a far cry from the way many ministry-team members operate, where outside the meeting they make decisions within their own silo without considering the success of the whole—a perspective sure to cause turf battles, conflicts, and misunderstandings.

Team members may or may not work on the same project. Teams are committed to the same mission but not necessarily the same project. A church staff team made up of directors of key ministries is committed to a mission that must be integrated across departmental lines. On the other hand, a youth ministry team may be focused on a single ministry or project.

Teams are not "leadership by committee." Committees are a terrible way to lead—someone must be the team leader or coach. Good leaders practice collaborative decision making so there is common ownership and buy in. Good leaders bring proposals to their teams (or ask others to do so) for discussion, robust dialogue, tweaking, and ultimate agreement. But good leaders *lead*.

H. I. MOMENT

What are your expectations of a team and how have they been met or not met on the team(s) you are on? Which of the fallacies discussed can you relate to?

H. I. DEFINITION

A high-impact ministry team is a group of missionally aligned and healthy individuals working strategically together under good leadership toward common objectives, with accountability for results.

CHARACTERISTICS OF HIGH-IMPACT TEAMS

Whether you serve on a church team, a mission team, a senior team, or a midlevel team, there are common elements that will move your team from average to high impact.

High-impact teams commit to a common mission. A team is not a team simply because it is called one. Healthy teams are based on a definable, well-articulated, passionately held common mission. In fact, you cannot have a high-impact team without passionate ownership of a common mission.

A key reason teams do not function well is the absence of a defined mission. In the absence of mission clarity, a team will find some other glue to hold it together, but the team will not be very effective because it does not have a central focus.

I once worked for a Christian organization made up of good people. The Executive Leadership Team of about twenty people met monthly. We didn't have a clearly articulated mission or focus. Thus, the team's function was to share what God was doing in our lives (which I didn't want to do since I had little in common with many of my teammates), what was happening in our ministries (which was interesting but not compelling since little we did was integrated), and to pray together (general prayers about general things). I did not enjoy these meetings! This was not a true team. There was no focus. We were not aligned.

Contrast that with the senior team I currently serve on, where we are deeply missional, do all we can to ensure alignment of ministries, discuss the big issues that drive our missional agenda, know one another, are pulling in the same direction, and are passionate about our mission. The contrast between the two teams—and their results—could not be greater.

If your team wants to see significant results, the glue that holds you together must be a well-articulated mission that you are all passionate about.

H. I. MOMENT

Does your team have a clear, meaningful mission you hold passionately? Do all members of your team buy into your stated mission? If not, it is critical that you develop a common mission as part of your study of this book. (If you need help doing this, see part 2 of *High-Impact Church Boards*, which deals with intentional leadership around mission, vision, values, and preferred future.)

High-impact team members align their individual ministries to their common mission. A common dysfunction of ministries is the lack of correlation among various departments. It is not unusual in church staff meetings for members to report their ministry's happenings without attention to concrete alignment *among* ministries. While all the parts may be good, they are also isolated.

High-impact teams reject that kind of silo mentality. It takes more time and energy to be aligned, but the results are a quantum leap from the outcomes of disparate ministries. Good leaders and teams take the harder road because it yields greater ministry impact.

A characteristic of good team leaders is that they insist on ministry alignment around common mission. In fact, the foundational reason we develop teams is to ensure this happens.

High-impact teams commit to the values, practices, and commitments of the organization at large. Integration means all members are committed to a set of common factors. One of the reasons many teams and organizations are not more effective is that they are not on the same page regarding foundational principles. For example, the mission organization I lead (ReachGlobal) has a mission, a set of ten guiding principles, a central ministry focus, and a defined culture. No one moves into leadership without complete buy in with these four areas. In fact, a person cannot join the organization in a ministry position without agreement in these four areas. Healthy teams commit to common ownership of the organizational values, practices, and commitments.

High-impact teams believe in the complementary use of gifts. Why bother to build and lead a team? A central reason is that healthy teams get far more done in a more creative and synergistic manner than one person could ever do alone. I am fascinated that God designated the senior leadership of the church as teams (elders and overseers, Acts 20) and not as individuals. When the early church sent missionaries, they sent a team (Barnabas and Paul, Acts 13). When the early church designed a ministry to take care of the widows and the poor, it created a team (deacons, Acts 6). This is a recognition that God gives various gifts to people and that the team is strongest when they work in concert with one another.

The senior team I sit on has six members. Bill, the president, is one of the most relational people I have ever met; he uses that God-given ability to choose great team members and bring people together across the denomination. He is also a "maximizer"[1] who always looks for ways to leverage ministry impact. Steve is the most intentional person I know, a great mentor and coach, a man who can shepherd any process toward its intended conclusion. Fritz combines strong relational skills with the ability to build team and cast vision for the ministries he oversees. He brings a deep passion for spiritual dependence to the senior team and the team he leads. Jot contributes great administrative gifts and oversees finances, business, and legal matters. Alvin combines strong strategic gifts with a passion to bring biblical diversity to our organization. I am described as one who can envision the future, cast vision, and communicate effectively.

Separately, we all have strong competencies. However, the combined strengths of the six members create a powerful entity where our gifts complement each other and create something exponentially greater than their sum. This has a compounding effect on the end product of our leadership.

A belief in the complementary use of our gifts also means that we willingly put those gifts into play whether they involve our ministry areas or some other part of the organization. We do not come to the team as representatives of our turf but rather as leaders who think of the whole. When we are looking at organizational issues, each of us willingly takes on responsibilities that are not directly "ours" but that will help drive the agenda of the ministry at large.

High-impact teams allow members to speak into each other's ministries, methods, and results. This is a logical extension of the characteristics we've described so far. Because team is all about mission, because we are about alignment, because we believe in the complementary use of gifts, and because we care more about the whole than our parts, we allow others to speak into our areas of ministry without being defensive or protective.

I remember when the senior team I serve on decided to form a truly interdependent team. Until that time I had operated fairly independently. I was accountable to the president but not necessarily to colleagues. I exercised huge freedom in my areas of responsibility. Then we started talking about forming an interdependent team around our mission, values, and preferred future.

I knew what the others knew. If we were going to go from independent departments to an integrated ministry, I would need to submit to the team—and they would have to do the same. Being a strong leader with strong opinions and convictions, I had a tough time submitting my piece of the turf to the leadership group. But it was absolutely the right thing to do, so I did it. And so did my colleagues.

There is a price to be paid if you truly desire a high-impact team. Healthy team membership demands our time, a commitment to a common mission, commitment to one another and alignment with others, a release of our independence, a focus that is wider than our personal ministry, and a submission of our gifts for the good of the whole. But the payoff is far greater than the price. Besides, it is biblical! None of us in ministry ought to be operating as lone rangers without the humility to work with, listen to, and learn from others.

High-impact teams are led by healthy leaders who love to develop, empower, and release team members. Healthy teams are not possible without a leader who has enough self-confidence to recruit highly competent individuals without being threatened by their strength.

A word to pastors here, of whom I have been one: We can be some of the most insecure folks in leadership because we are often unable to separate who we are from what we do. In the secular world it is not uncommon for staff members to have a serious work disagreement and keep it confined to work. Opposing attorneys, for instance, may battle it out in the courtroom and then go to the pub for a drink afterward. But because what we do becomes our identity, pastors are easily offended or become defensive when someone takes issue with something related to ministry; we personalize it rather than take it as an opinion about how we might do something differently. Like many of you, I have been guilty of the same.

Healthy leaders are not defensive or threatened. They have developed an attitude of "nothing to prove, nothing to lose." They do not need to be right all the time, can separate who they are from what they do, and want what is best for the ministry they lead. Thus there is no need to be defensive when someone critiques or suggests alternative methods. They are also willing to surround themselves with people who are more gifted than they are; after all, the team effort is not about the leader but the *mission*.

Healthy leaders also empower rather than control. The need to micromanage is a sign of leaders who are defensive and threatened by other's competencies—or who believe something will be done incorrectly if they don't control it. (If that is the case, the leaders hired or recruited the wrong person.)

Healthy leaders believe in and practice collegial, collaborative leadership. They allow robust dialogue and debate and help the group come to common conclusions and commitments. Good leaders hire good people, define the boundaries of their work, and release them to get the job done. Good leaders are also willing to give those who report to them honest and helpful feedback so they can grow in their responsibilities.

Good leaders realize they will maximize the impact of the ministry only as they empower good people, cheer them on, and give them credit for what they do.

One of the reasons I have such great regard for my leader, Bill, is his ability to put together a strong team, allow that team to grapple with key directional issues, and then release us to get the job done. He is not jealous of his position or authority; in turn, we don't want his job! I have worked for leaders who were threatened by others, and it was not pretty. Bill understands what it means to be a great team leader, and it is liberating.

For those of us who lead teams, there is no substitute for continuing to grow as healthy, effective, empowering leaders. People love to work for leaders who have those characteristics and will be exceedingly loyal to them.

High-impact teams orient toward execution. Some organizations are high on planning but short on execution. Good teams are results oriented. Members of high-impact teams focus on developing the best possible strategies for the organization at large so its mission is fulfilled. While there is an important element of communication and coordination in team meetings—so the right hand knows what the left hand is doing—the real work of teams is strategizing the best way to move the organization (or their part of the organization) forward. Teams should devote a significant portion of their meeting time to problems that need solving, opportunities that can be leveraged, and planning for the future. This is always done in the context of their organization's mission, values, and preferred future.

Team leaders must ensure discussions lead to concrete proposals that define who is responsible for doing what. These decisions are recorded in team minutes and form the basis for updates at the next meeting. If this one practice were followed, teams would be far more productive than they usually are.

High-impact teams are composed of emotionally healthy people. Beware of whom you put on your team! Healthy individuals make teamwork a joy. Unhealthy individuals kill an otherwise good team.

Emotional Intelligence, often labeled EQ,[2] is the ability to understand ourselves, know what drives us, accurately see how others perceive us, and understand how we relate to others. EQ also measures whether we have the relational skill to work with others while being "self-defining" and allowing others to speak into our lives. Good EQ includes openness to others' opinions, lack of defensiveness, sensitivity to others, the ability to release others rather than control them, freedom for constructive and robust dialogue, and the willingness to abide by common decisions.

Signs of poor EQ include the inability to listen to others, defensiveness, unawareness of how we come across, lack of sensitivity to others' feelings, an inability to deal constructively with conflict, a drive to control others, narcissism, and the need to have our own way.

There is a growing awareness of the need to hire people who are competent, who have character, and who fit the culture of our organizations. However, we pay too little attention to the EQ of those we recruit to be members of our teams.

It is possible for people to have great competence but to have low EQ and leave relational havoc in their wakes. Don't put them on your team! In fact, if these people cannot be helped to become healthy, they probably should not be an employee of your ministry no matter how competent they are; the relational damage they cause inside and outside the organization is too high. (The alternative is to put them in a spot where they will do the least damage to others.)

High-impact teams are created deliberately. When you add people to a team you are building, you need to consider a number of questions:

- Do they have good EQ?
- Can they play at or above the level of other team members?
- Do they have a skill(s) that will complement the team?
- Are they team players?
- Can they contribute to the whole rather than simply guard their turf?
- Do they fully embrace the mission and values of the organization?

- Do the other members of the team think they will fit well?
- Do they have the expertise for the ministry in which they will participate?
- Do they understand the implications of joining the team and the expectations of a team member?

H. I. BEST PRACTICE

When adding people to an existing team, it is wise to allow current team members to interview them and help the leader determine whether there is a good fit. Each person you add will change the team dynamics. Securing the buy in of existing members can help the process proceed more smoothly.

The higher the level at which the team operates, the more important it is to carefully vet new members. If you add to a high-level team someone who cannot contribute at the same level as the other team members, you have reduced the team's output. The other members will notice the difference, and the change will become demotivating. The same response would occur if you added a highly competent member who was unwilling to act as a full team member.

One way to ensure a good fit is to allow a potential new member to serve on an invitation basis. That gives the team the opportunity to observe the potential contribution without committing fully. The invitation should not guarantee permanent service on the team.

Team members should serve at the invitation of the team leader. Stating up front that team positions are not permanent lets members know that service on a team is not guaranteed forever. Take, for instance, the senior leadership team of a church staff. Someone who plays effectively on that team at one period of a church's history may not serve as effectively as the church grows. The team leader must have the prerogative to add or subtract team members if that is best for the organization. If the organization outgrows the capacity of team members or they become disengaged from the work of the team, they should no longer serve.

Also, position alone should not determine who is on a specific team. Competence, capacity, and contribution should also be considered. The senior team of ReachGlobal currently has ten members, plus me as the leader. Some members are there because they serve in senior positions of the organization. Others, however, are on the team because their competence and capacity are such that I choose to have them at the table — it would be foolish of me not to include them.

High-impact team leaders carefully plan and execute meetings. Few things are more irritating than being required to attend meetings that are carelessly planned and poorly led. Leaders effectively set the tone for their team by the care they model in designing meaningful agendas, keeping meetings on target, and ensuring time is well spent. When this doesn't happen, team members receive the message that "this is not that important," and they will not take their roles seriously.

Too many leaders underprepare for team meetings, considering them a distraction from more important issues. Team time is not an ancillary to a leader's priorities. It is central. Team time is when leaders remind people of mission. It is when they plan, solve problems, and dream around the preferred future of the organization — or the slice of the organization they represent. It is a time to pray together and learn together.

One of my goals in designing team meetings is that no one leaves without having learned something new. Another goal is that everyone is reminded of the mission.

High-impact teams encourage robust dialogue. One of the reasons team leaders must have a healthy EQ is that healthy teams encourage honest, frank dialogue about all issues (with the exception of personal attacks). In our organization we constantly say we want no elephants in the room; if elephants exist, they need to be named and discussed.

This does not work for insecure leaders who easily become defensive. Defensiveness kills robust dialogue because it sends a message that "this topic" is out of bounds. One can judge the relative health of a team by the number of elephants in the room — the topics that are instinctively known to be out of bounds.

The ability to engage in honest and frank dialogue signals that trust has been established among members, allowing them to evaluate one another's areas of responsibility without taking umbrage. Team members will develop this frankness only when they see their leader encourage it through an open posture.

Defensiveness is about "me," while robust dialogue is about the mission. Ultimately we are about the mission, so we need to put away our petty insecurities for the sake of the mission.

H. I. DEFINITION

Robust dialogue is the ability to discuss freely and with candor any issue of organizational or ministry importance, while refraining from personal attacks or driving hidden agendas, in order to further the effectiveness and mission of the organization.

Because the ability to engage in robust dialogue is so critical, it is important to understand what it is—and what it is not. Robust dialogue is the ability to discuss any issue with candor in order to further the effectiveness and mission of the organization. Robust dialogue is honest conversation about critical issues. It is dialogue, not attacks or pronouncements. Some people try to drive their own agendas in the *guise* of dialogue; it is clear from their questions and interactions that a critical and antagonistic spirit is behind their comments. This is neither honest (the agenda is not stated up front and the attitude behind it is not healthy), nor is it dialogue (what they really want is their way).

Robust dialogue is not a "free pass" to say anything we want to say in whatever spirit we want to say it. As Paul said in Ephesians 4, if our words are not constructive or edifying and our attitude one that wants the best for others, we should not speak. Robust dialogue helps the organization be more effective in accomplishing its mission. It is never an excuse to drive personal agendas or speak without love and respect.

Robust dialogue along with a high degree of trust are important components of healthy teams. I regularly meet individuals who long to serve on a healthy team with a healthy leader and healthy teammates. Where one finds that combination, there is great enthusiasm for the ministry and mission. Where it is absent, there is frustration and a lack of cooperation and alignment. The building of healthy teams is one of the most needed components in ministry today.

H. I. QUESTIONS FOR TEAM DISCUSSION

As you look over the fallacies of what a team is, are there any that you have held? Discuss your answers with team members.

On which of the team characteristics is your team strong and on which is it weak?

In your opinion, which of the team characteristics are hardest to carry out? Why?

On a scale of one to ten (with ten being the highest), how strong would you rate the team(s) you are on? Why?

CHAPTER TWO

THE POWER OF CLARITY

CHAPTER SUMMARY:

The single most important thing a leader does is provide maximum clarity to those they lead about what is important to the organization and how the organization is going to accomplish its mission. Achieving clarity is the most powerful accelerator toward ministry results and organizational alignment.

There are four areas where maximum clarity is critical:

- *Mission:* What we are ultimately committed to accomplishing
- *Guiding Principles:* How we are committed to operating
- *Central Ministry Focus:* What we need to be doing day in and day out to accomplish our mission
- *Preferred Culture:* The ethos we need to have to accomplish the first three areas

The goal of maximum clarity is to empower your staff to make ministry decisions in alignment with your core convictions and, in the process, provide for a high level of accountability. Leaders clarify the important issues so that healthy and productive people know how to proceed within the organization.

The "sandbox" is a simple tool that allows for alignment around ministry philosophy rather than methods.

Leading from the sandbox:

- Empowers good people
- Provides for accountability
- Allows you to deal with staff who don't play ball
- Has a high "get it" factor
- Helps you recruit and train people whose convictions are consistent with your organization's

---

The most important thing leaders do is provide maximum clarity to those they lead about the key priorities of the organization and how the organization is going to accomplish its mission. Without that understanding, personnel are left to their own devices to figure out what is important. Different people will come up with different answers, leaving the organization without a focused ministry.

Think about this: Without clarity, an organization will never be integrated or aligned (around what?), will not attract the best people (they want to know what they are giving their lives to), and will not know when it has achieved what it needs to do (what results are being sought?). Even leaders will not know where to lead their teams (because they don't know how to be intentional) or have a means of making directional decisions (there is no grid). Without addressing these issues, you will not be a high-impact leader and you will not lead a high-impact team. Achieving clarity is not necessarily easy, but getting there is the single most powerful accelerator toward ministry results and organizational alignment. The results are worth the time and effort.

The "sandbox" described in this chapter is a tool for helping you develop clarity for the ministry you lead. With that clarity in place, your leadership role becomes much easier because there is now focus and common direction for you, your team, and the entire organization. Maximum clarity changes the leadership and organizational equation in a huge way—for the good. It is a game changer!

SEEKING CLARITY

In 2004, I was appointed executive director of ReachGlobal, a global mission organization with more than five hundred individuals living in more than forty countries. The organization had grown rapidly in the past several decades under my wonderful predecessor, and it was focused on church planting. However, there was little alignment through the organization as a whole, or even agreement as to what questions we needed to answer. Part of this lack of alignment was a result of the tremendous growth that had come with the opening of dozens of new fields and the growth of creative-access ministries.

Being deeply committed to maximum empowerment as well as lines of accountability, I faced the challenge of articulating the big issues about which we needed agreement in order to release personnel to make decisions. I wanted to bring clarity in a way that resulted in empowerment and alignment throughout the global organization.

I want to be clear that my use of ReachGlobal as an illustration here should not be construed as criticism of past leadership or mission paradigm. Times change, leadership needs change, and I came into leadership at one of those junctures when a consolidation of gains needed to take place for the organization to be effective and healthy into the future.

Previously, there had not been a high degree of empowerment. In the absence of boundaries showing what was acceptable and unacceptable, leaders had to check with the international office to obtain approval for decisions. This is one of the many downsides of lack of clarity — people run the risk of making decisions that are not acceptable because the boundaries of what *is* acceptable have not been defined.

Over the first year I worked with senior staff and the board to clarify four areas that had to be defined if we were to empower our personnel while also maintaining accountability:

- *Mission:* what we were ultimately committed to accomplishing
- *Guiding principles:* how we were committed to operating

- *Central ministry focus:* what we needed to be doing day in and day out to accomplish our mission
- *Preferred culture of the organization:* what would make it possible to accomplish our mission

The process of articulating these areas led us to maximum clarity and can lead your organization there as well.

Clarity on mission. ReachGlobal had been operating with a mission statement different from that of its parent organization, the EFCA. Fortunately, the mission of the EFCA was clearly defined: "The mission of the EFCA is to glorify God by multiplying healthy churches among all people." The mission statement articulates central issues that became ours as well: "church," "multiplication," "health," and "all people." Thus, we brought the mission of the international ministries in line with the parent organization.

Clarity on guiding principles or values. Like many organizations, ours had a list of values that were not even remembered by leaders or personnel and did not directly influence how ministry was carried out. Values should provide significant guidance in how we do what we do; ours, while good, were too general to be useful in providing guidance. Hence, as we clarified values, we chose to call them "guiding principles" to drive home the fact that they were designed to actually *guide* everyone in the organization in how to make decisions and carry out ministry.

We defined ten guiding principles that every leader and all personnel are expected to live by. As you read the following list, note that they describe how personnel will approach ministry, and they are specific enough that it is possible for leaders to determine whether their team members are ministering in alignment with them.

REACHGLOBAL GUIDING PRINCIPLES

We are Word based and Spirit empowered. As a Word-based organization we are committed to ministry that aligns with God's Word. Spirit empowerment comes from intimacy with Christ, a deep commitment to prayer, watching where God is at work, and always listening to His voice.

We are team led and team driven. Believing that there is strength in teams and in the voice of multiple leaders, we are committed to a paradigm of team leadership under a gifted leader at each level of ReachGlobal ministry.

We believe that ministry personnel are more productive when they are deployed in ministry teams and in community with one another. We will build strong teams with healthy relationships wherever we deploy personnel.

We are partnership driven. We are committed to carrying out the Great Commission in partnership with local churches in the United States, national partners, and other evangelical organizations.

We recognize the biblical value of healthy cooperation with national partners. This includes the avoidance of paternalistic attitudes and a willingness to share appropriately in ministry decisions that affect both parties. Healthy partnerships include mutual cooperation without either party losing its identity or ability to work toward its intended objectives.

We empower personnel. We are permission granting — within agreed-upon parameters — rather than permission withholding. We help personnel discover their strengths and deploy them in ways that maximize their gifting and abilities.

We practice entrepreneurial thinking. In global ministry, one size does not fit all and, while our mission remains constant, the strategies to complete the mission vary and change. We always look for "best practices" and better ways to fulfill our mission.

We measure effectiveness. ReachGlobal is committed to being accountable to EFCA churches and supporters for tangible ministry results. A commitment to effective ministry requires the accountability of measurements.

We do multiplication rather than addition. Understanding that the task of world evangelism is huge and that mission workers and resources are limited, we are committed to strategies of multiplication over addition. We are facilitators and ministry coaches who come alongside national leaders to empower and train them.

We are a learning organization. ReachGlobal is committed to providing ongoing training and equipping of personnel in life and ministry skills. ReachGlobal will only be as good as the leaders who provide leadership at each level. We will find, equip, and deploy those who have the gifts of leadership and who have proven leadership effectiveness.

We resource for maximum ministry. A well-resourced organization is more likely to be an effective organization. It is the responsibility of all ReachGlobal personnel to participate in the threefold resourcing of personnel, strategy, and finances.

We are holistic and integrated in approach. Historically, missions have emphasized the biblical mandate of ministering to the whole person in the name of Christ. This includes ministries of compassion, education, and other ministry platforms in addition to those of evangelism and church planting. A distinctive of ReachGlobal is that all ministries are integrated into the goal of multiplying healthy churches.

Notice that each guiding principle is followed by a definition of its meaning. These explanations have been carefully crafted and edited over time to identify what the guiding principle means and how it affects ministry.

As you can imagine, not everyone in as large an organization as ours agreed with all the guiding principles. However, leadership was absolutely committed to them, and I spent the better part of eighteen months meeting with staff to discuss these principles, answer questions, and be the prime evangelist for them—something I continue to do.

Today there is no question in the minds of our personnel that we are committed to these guiding principles and that all of us are expected to live by them. These principles inform everything we do.

H. I. MOMENT

Does your organization have a set of guiding principles that guide personnel and ministries?

Are they sufficiently clear so there is no question in anyone's mind as to what is expected? (For additional information on developing values or guiding principles, see *High-Impact Church Boards*.)

Clarity on central ministry focus. An organization's central ministry focus is the most important thing it does to fulfill its mission. The question you need to ask is, "What is the one thing all of us must be committed to doing that, if done consistently and well, will ensure we maximize our ministry opportunity?" Our version of that question was, "Given our mission of multiplying healthy churches among all people in a global environment, what do we need to focus on to maximize our opportunity to fulfill that mission?"

One obvious answer would have been the traditional one: Our missionaries should concentrate on planting churches. But how many churches can five hundred missionaries plant at any one time? Furthermore, one of our guiding principles is, "We do multiplication rather than addition." This answer was inconsistent with that principle. Therefore, we identified one central focus with two applications: "The central ministry focus of ReachGlobal is to develop, empower, and release healthy ReachGlobal personnel and to develop, empower, and release healthy national leaders."

How one answers the central ministry focus question has a huge implication for the effectiveness of one's ministry. It is our conviction that the key to our effectiveness is having the best possible trained and deployed personnel, and the key to multiplying healthy churches is to focus like a laser on developing, empowering, and releasing healthy national leaders who can multiply churches far faster and more effectively than we can.

What this means practically is that everywhere we deploy personnel, we come alongside national leaders, determine with them what they most need to be successful in the multiplication of healthy churches, and serve them by meeting these needs. We are not there to do what they can do but rather to empower them to reach their own people. In places where there are no believers to come alongside, we engage in apostolic ministry: doing evangelism and developing leaders who from the beginning can lead any fellowships that are established.

The central ministry focus is the one thing that everyone in the organization must be committed to doing all the time. For many ministries this will be about equipping and releasing people into ministry.

A parenthesis for church leaders. The concept of focusing on developing, empowering, and releasing others is one of the central themes of the New Testament. This is what Christ did with the twelve disciples, and it is what

Paul called church leaders to do in Ephesians 4. Paul said the focus of church leaders' ministries is "to prepare God's people for works of service, so that the body of Christ may be built up until we all reach unity in the faith and in the knowledge of the Son of God and become mature, attaining to the whole measure of the fullness of Christ" (verses 12-13).

The key to our ministry, according to Paul, is releasing the whole body into ministry, rather than doing the ministry ourselves. One of the greatest dysfunctions of the church today is that of "professional ministry," where we hire experts to do ministry rather than equip the body of Christ to do it. I have no doubt this is one reason local churches have so little impact on their communities and why there is so little difference between how Christians and non-Christians live. In verse 12, Paul indicated that people do not become mature unless they are actively using their gifts, and he said congregations are not mature until everyone is in the game. There are churches that live this out, but way too few. If every congregation lived out Ephesians 4:12, releasing people into ministry in accordance with how God had gifted them, the local church would be the revolutionary force God designed it to be.

Clarity on the preferred culture. ReachGlobal had now defined its mission, its guiding principles, and its central focus. The final question was about what preferred culture would allow us to accomplish our mission.

Why is defining your preferred culture so important? Because if you focus on the wrong things, you negate your efforts in the first three areas. For instance, with the world population at 6.5 billion and an unreached population of around 6 billion, it would seem reasonable that a mission organization would focus on deploying as many missionaries as possible. Therefore, we might have chosen "numbers" as critical to our preferred culture. However, defining our desired culture as the number of missionaries on the field might, in fact, hurt us. Why? If many of the missionaries are unhealthy or dysfunctional there is no way the organization will be healthy or able to train healthy national workers, deploy healthy teams, or end up with healthy churches. The preferred culture one commits to has consequences — good or bad.

The preferred culture for ReachGlobal had to be "health" if we were to get to the multiplication of *healthy* churches (note that *health* was a key word in both the mission and the central focus). Our preferred-culture statement is, "ReachGlobal is committed to establishing a culture of health: healthy personnel, working on healthy teams, training healthy leaders to multiply healthy churches." Without a preferred culture — in this case "health" — we would not be able to achieve our mission on an ongoing basis.

Once we had defined "health" as our preferred culture, we then formatted all of our recruiting, team building, training, leadership development, and church materials to fit that culture. We had to infuse the culture of health throughout the organization. This means we had to define a healthy missionary, a healthy team, a healthy leader, and a healthy church. It also meant that recruiting, assessment, training, and evaluation had to include a significant component that measured health.

In the next chapter, we'll focus on the culture of organizations, and in chapter 4, you will have an opportunity to define the culture of your organization.

LEADING FROM THE SANDBOX

In ReachGlobal, we want our staff to have great satisfaction in ministry and to be free to use their wiring and gifts to maximum effect while we make the greatest impact for Christ through the multiplication of healthy churches. We want our teams to be empowered, aligned, and accountable. So we took our mission, guiding principles, central ministry focus, and preferred culture and used them as the four sides of what I call our organization's "sandbox." I think it would be fair to say that everyone in our far-flung organization knows about the sandbox and what it represents.

Almost all of us can remember a time when we were young and played in a sandbox. Creativity and work were synonymous in the sandbox. You could build whatever you wanted and let your imagination go. Whether you were building castles or making roads for a Barbie or G. I. Joe, it was a great place to be. But you quickly learned the sand-box was only fun as long as two things were true: You got along with those you were playing with, and the sand stayed in the box.

Like those early years when we actually had fun in our "work," the same should be true today. Leading a team is all about understanding the giftings of those we lead and then releasing them to play to their strengths, literally to "play" in their ministry. But for this to work, there must be clearly defined boundaries that we ask our people to stay within—and they need to play well with their fellow teammates.

We communicated to our personnel that they have maximum freedom to "play inside the sandbox," to make ministry decisions consistent with the areas defined by the sides of the sandbox (empowerment). We will also hold them accountable for staying *inside* the sandbox (alignment) and carrying out the mandate provided by the sides of the sandbox (accountability).

There is no question in the minds of anyone in ReachGlobal as to the commitment of its leaders to the four sides of the sandbox. This is who we are. This is what we are committed to. This is our central ministry focus. This is our mission. This is our preferred culture. These are our guiding principles. Everywhere I go, I unpack the principles, commitments, and implications of the sandbox. I lead from the sandbox.

My central job as a leader of ReachGlobal is to provide clarity about who we are, how we do what we do, what we concentrate on, what our preferred culture is, and where we are going. Those elements are all contained in the sandbox picture.

ReachGlobal Sandbox

We exist to glorify God by multiplying
healthy churches among all people

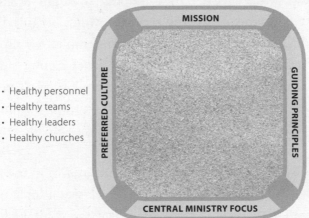

- Healthy personnel
- Healthy teams
- Healthy leaders
- Healthy churches

MISSION

PREFERRED CULTURE

GUIDING PRINCIPLES

CENTRAL MINISTRY FOCUS

- Word based and Spirit empowered
- Team led and team driven
- Partnership driven
- Empowered personnel
- Entrepreneurial thinking
- Measure effectiveness
- Multiplication not addition
- Learning organization
- Resourced well
- Holistic and integrated in approach

To develop, empower, and release healthy
ReachGlobal personnel and healthy
national leaders

The sandbox ensures maximum clarity. Leaders clarify the important issues so good people know how to proceed within the organization. The discipline of defining your sandbox requires you to come to grips with mission, values, central ministry focus, and preferred culture. If you cannot define these four key missional elements, and if everyone in leadership cannot articulate them and be in agreement with them, you are living with dangerous ambiguity rather than missional clarity.

Frankly, this is the key difference between ministries that could be classified as good or nice and those that could be called excellent and mission driven. For instance, show me a flourishing church that has a significant track record and you will find leaders who are very clear on who they are, where they are going, and what their preferred culture is.

This clarity allows your personnel to identify their priorities as well. Interestingly, some ReachGlobal personnel did not want to live within the four sides of our sandbox, and they transitioned out. No one joins our organization today who is not completely in sync with the four areas we've defined as the central description of who we are. Our sandbox provides maximum clarity for leaders, recruits, staff, church partners, and national partners.

The sandbox helps people "get it." The sandbox paradigm is simple to understand, yet profound in its implications. Many organizations are either vague about what they are about or so complicated no one understands it. If the average person in our ministries cannot simply and quickly articulate what we are about, we have done them (and our ministries) a great disservice. The sandbox takes a complex ministry (and most ministries are) and simplifies it to four areas that, when taken as a whole, quickly explain the ministry.

Most of our personnel have responded with enthusiasm to the four aspects of the sandbox. First, they appreciate the clarity. People want to know their boundaries. Second, they appreciate the empowerment and the freedom to use their creativity and gifts. Third, they appreciate that success has been defined and they know how they will be evaluated. Fourth, and most important, they get it. Not only has the sandbox brought clarity to our own personnel, but it is also bringing understanding to the thousands of partners and church leaders who support or interact with ReachGlobal.

The same can happen for entire congregations if leaders develop their own sandbox for the church and use this simple tool to communicate their ministry priorities. In chapter 4, you will see examples of "sandboxes" from different types of organizations.

The sandbox allows for alignment around ministry philosophy rather than methods. In the past thirty years, the world has gone from black-and-white to color. In many ways it mirrors the transition from the preglobalized world to the globalized world. I define the differences this way:

BLACK-AND-WHITE VERSUS COLOR WORLDS

Black-and-White World	Color World
• One size fits all	• Multiple needs, multiple answers
• Few options	• Many options
• Uniformity	• Customization

• Command and control	• Empowerment
• Top down	• Flat
• We are the experts	• There are many experts
• The world is big	• The world is small
• Uniformity around strategy	• Uniformity around values
• Jobs based on need	• Work based on gifting
• Information flows through hierarchy	• Information flows where needed

Do not underestimate the significance of the shift from the black-and-white world to the color world. We live in a different world than we did thirty years ago. However, many ministries have not recognized that the world has changed, and they have not changed to meet the challenges of a color world.

Many missions organizations face serious issues in this regard. Some people who have served long years resonate with the black-and-white world and resist change. Those coming in today are looking for organizations that live in the color world. The two cultures cannot coexist. A mission agency must either transition from black-and-white to color or face a slow slide into decline. The same can be said for many churches that have not grasped the changing landscape.

The core uniformity in today's world is around a common set of values, commitments, culture, or philosophy. Methods will vary by context (different situations require different approaches). Empowerment means that people need to be able to make decisions based on their situation. If they have maximum clarity on ministry philosophy as defined by your sandbox, they can freely decide among any number of methods that are consistent with who you are.

Our organization used to insist on alignment around methodology, but that is impossible in the twenty-first century. Today, we have more alignment than ever before *and* more diversity of methods as we work in seventy-five countries, all with different needs. If you lead a church team, you know that the needs of different groups span a wide spectrum. With a well-defined sandbox, you can allow for freedom in methodology while staying aligned around the core issues.

H. I. MOMENT

Does your ministry live more in the black-and-white world or in the color world? What factors support your conclusion? Discuss your views as a ministry team.

The sandbox empowers people. High-impact leaders do not control those they lead. They identify boundaries the organization is committed to and then release people to find solutions consistent with those boundaries. Once you have provided clarity, you can release people to find solutions that work within their contexts.

This does not mean leaders do not give input when needed; it does change the kind of input we give. When leaders in my organization ask if they can do something, I rarely answer with a yes or no. Rather, I ask if it is in alignment with our sandbox. Then I probe (good leaders ask lots of questions) to help staff discern the wisdom of the option they are considering.

In large organizations like ours, the definitions and boundaries of our sandbox also help practitioners in far-flung places develop ministry plans consistent with our commitments. Their supervisors encourage them to think through methodology that will work in their contexts and give them freedom and empowerment to make those decisions (with appropriate coaching and mentoring).

Whether your ministry is large or small, empowerment is possible only when there is great understanding about core missional elements. Once you have those in place and there is agreement on the implications those elements bring, good people can be empowered to accomplish ministry in alignment with your mission, values, central ministry focus, and culture.

The sandbox provides for maximum accountability. Empowerment and accountability are two sides of the same coin. Once you have maximum clarity, you also have objective ways to measure results. ReachGlobal can measure health results, adherence to the central ministry focus, alignment to the guiding principles, and multiplication of healthy churches.

Furthermore, the Key Result Areas (KRAs) of ministry teams and the Annual Ministry Plans (AMPs) (which we'll discuss in chapter 7) must both be in alignment with the sandbox and provide for ways to measure annual ministry results.

The sandbox allows you to deal with staff who don't play ball. Because the sandbox defines who you are, it also allows you to identify and deal with those who choose not to live in alignment. In the absence of these guidelines, it may be difficult to identify what you are unhappy about when faced with an uncooperative team member. The sandbox solves that problem.

Lack of alignment by staff who refuse to play ball hurts your ministry significantly. Their continued independence sends a powerful message that you are not serious about what you say. Whether their indifference is active or passive, it is like the drag of an anchor.

With the sandbox, ReachGlobal has an objective tool to address staff members who step outside the boundaries; we deal with them on the basis that they are violating the commitments of the ministry. For us, this includes the culture side of the sandbox with our emphasis on health. When an unhealthy individual is causing relational chaos or other difficulties on a team, we act in a redemptive way (and we are usually successful) to bring health to the person and, subsequently, to the team. When that is not possible, we will help the individual move out of ReachGlobal. To do otherwise is to hurt other team members and, ultimately, the entire organization.

Many Christian organizations live with significant relational pain and conflict when they are unable to deal with unhealthy or uncooperative staff members who hurt the team and work at cross purposes with the rest of the staff. In the absence of maximum clarity, it is difficult for even good leaders to hold these individuals accountable for their attitudes, behavior, and ministry results.

The sandbox helps you recruit and train people whose convictions are consistent with your own. There is great pain in finding that the wonderful person you recruited a few months or years ago does not really fit your culture or your ministry. Every time that happens, we ask ourselves, "How could we have avoided the error?" One way to minimize this risk is to be incredibly defining on the front end.

For instance, if mission candidates look at ReachGlobal and think they will have a career planting and pastoring churches, they will quickly realize we are about equipping and releasing *nationals* for leadership positions. If their preferred situation is to minister by themselves, they will realize that we are about teamwork, and our organization is not a good fit for them. The more understanding you have about who you are as a ministry and the better you can articulate that, the better chance you have of recruiting people who resonate with who you are. And when it comes to training your people, the sandbox provides a simple and uncomplicated tool that allows everyone to hear the same thing.

BUILDING YOUR OWN SANDBOX

The sandbox has four sides: mission, guiding principles or values, central ministry focus, and the preferred culture. Start thinking about what your four sides would look like if you had a sandbox. Chapter 4 will guide you through the process of constructing a sandbox that fits your ministry.

H. I. QUESTIONS FOR TEAM DISCUSSION

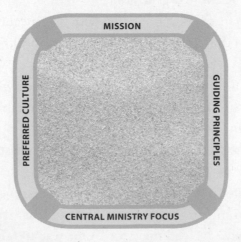

In which areas does your ministry have maximum clarity and in which areas is there a lack of maximum clarity?

What is the connection between the sandbox and the twin sides of the same coin, accountability and empowerment?

If you were to take a stab at defining your central ministry focus, what would it be?

Where is your ministry living in the black-and-white world and where is it living in the color world? Do you see the need to reevaluate practices of your ministry on the basis of this concept?

Do the values of your ministry provide actual direction to staff and leadership and are they clearly known by all? Is there a need to evaluate your values or how they are defined?

CHAPTER THREE

DEFINING YOUR CULTURE

CHAPTER SUMMARY:

Every organization has a unique defining culture. Organizational culture is the unspoken ethos of a group of people, including its beliefs, social behaviors, practices, attitudes, values, and traditions—all of which contribute to a collective way of thinking and practice.

Culture is positive or negative, never neutral. Leaders must be acutely aware of the culture of their organizations.

Culture has a direct effect not only on people but also on the organization's ability to flex and meet rapidly changing opportunities and environments.

Many organizational cultures suffer from one or more of the five dysfunctions of ministry organizations:

1. Control
2. Bureaucracy
3. Ambiguity
4. Professional ministry
5. Mistrust

You do not need to settle for these dysfunctions or the culture you currently have but can define the culture you want to develop and systematically move in that direction. Changing your culture takes time, and senior leadership must practice and be the champions of the preferred culture. Consistency of the senior leader's message over time becomes a key factor in creating a new culture within an organization.

Leaders who "live the sandbox" demonstrate their deep resolve that the culture defined by the sandbox becomes the culture of the organization.

Every organization has a unique defining culture. When we have been in an organization for a while, we aren't aware of its culture—we have become part of it. However, it is worth thinking about because the culture will have an impact—positive or negative—on ministry. Leaders, especially, must be acutely aware of the culture of their organizations. They must recognize that how they lead and how they define their sandbox will influence the organization's culture.

H. I. DEFINITION

Organizational culture is the unspoken ethos of a group of people, including its beliefs, social behaviors, practices, attitudes, values, and traditions — all of which contribute to a collective way of thinking and practice.

As you ponder this definition, recognize that culture is not neutral. Beliefs, social behaviors, practices, attitudes, values, and traditions affect who your organization is and how people act. They also change the organization's ability to achieve its mission and attract and retain good people, and they carry enormous implications for issues such as empowerment and accountability.

A TRUE STORY

I recently received a call from a highly skilled, successful, veteran missionary who is seriously considering leaving full-time missions, getting a job to support himself in Asia, and coaching church-planting efforts in his spare time.

For twenty-four years he worked for a well-known evangelical mission agency. He had great relationships, but the agency was so traditional he concluded there wasn't a place for him anymore. He is convinced that missions today is primarily about coming alongside nationals and equipping them to plant indigenous churches — something they can do better than Westerners (he is right). The mission he worked for is still operating in an old cultural model where Western missionaries plant the churches and supervise nationals.

A year ago he transferred to another well-known mission where he was to oversee church-planting efforts in a creative-access country. Yet after visiting fifteen of the church-planting teams, he found that not one of them had a plan that would produce healthy church plants — and all their work was dependent on Westerners.

The situations he described in these two organizations arose from their culture; while he loves the people in the organizations, their cultures (practices, beliefs, traditions, attitudes, values, and social behaviors) were deeply discouraging and, in his view, counterproductive to their goals.

As a long-time consultant to local churches, I have seen the gamut of healthy and unhealthy cultures. I have visited churches where the prevailing culture is critical and harsh, and others where there is grace and freedom. I have seen both controlling and empowering leaders, staffs who are in alignment and those that are siloed.

A friend of mine consults with parachurch ministries in the United States. Several years ago he was asked to do an organizational audit of one of the best-known ministries in the nation. He interviewed all the top ministry leaders and discovered a great deal of unhappiness because of the controlling, dogmatic nature of the senior leader.

In his report to the leader, the consultant told him that he was likely to lose most of his top echelon of leaders over the next few years because of the leadership culture of the ministry. The leader laughed and said, "No one leaves this ministry." He was wrong. Over the next several years, each of the senior leaders left for opportunities where they could better use their gifts and abilities.

The bottom line is that culture matters. The best ministry people will not stay long-term in unhealthy cultures. Like my missionary friend, they value the time they have to make a difference for the kingdom, and they will not invest their lives where the culture does not support the desired returns.

Organizational culture also has a direct influence on an organization's ability to flex and meet rapidly changing opportunities and environments. Mission agencies with a traditional, change-averse culture that are still using Western missionaries to plant churches one-by-one are missing the mark. They could be seeing multiples of church-planting results if they concentrated on developing, empowering, and releasing healthy national workers.[1] Their culture is preventing them from being effective. Likewise, church cultures that are controlling and do not empower and release good leaders and team members are compromising themselves missionally.

H. I. MOMENT

Take fifteen minutes and jot down one-word descriptors of the organization you are a part of — taking into account its beliefs, social behaviors, practices, attitudes, values, and traditions. Then write a one-sentence description of its culture. When you are with the rest of your team, share your definition of the culture.

_____

_____

_____

_____

_____

FIVE COMMON DYSFUNCTIONS OF MINISTRY ORGANIZATIONS

As I have consulted with churches and ministry organizations and helped them identify their cultures, I have recognized five common dysfunctions that exert a tremendous negative effect on ministries.

1. The dysfunction of control. Control is the opposite of empowerment. Empowerment releases people within specified boundaries to use their gifts and abilities for maximum ministry impact. All too often, leaders or the organization's culture mitigate against empowerment and exercise stringent control over people and methodology.

Control is not always overt, but it has the same consequences as if it were. My own organization used to insist there were only a few ways to do church planting. People who were entrepreneurial and tried other methodologies were sometimes marginalized because they did not use the prescribed methods. Beliefs and practices were the controlling factor.

In many local churches, congregations have the sense they must control their leaders, insisting that all decisions come back to the congregation for approval. Many leadership boards believe the staff might do something unwise if they are not controlled. Staff members often believe they need to control volunteers to guard the quality of ministry—and on it goes.

The worst form of control comes in the form of a church "boss" who has informal veto power over any ministry decision, or an insecure leader who must micromanage staff and activities out of his or her need to know everything, have a hand in everything, and take credit for everything.

One of the strongest themes running through this book is that healthy leaders and healthy teams empower people for ministry and encourage them to play to their strengths in alignment with their gifts. Jesus empowered His disciples, and the leaders He left behind were told to empower and release others—the theme of Ephesians 4. Leaders determine whether their culture empowers its people or controls them.

2. The dysfunction of bureaucracy. Bureaucracy is a first cousin to control. I define bureaucracy as unnecessary "tollbooths" that need to be negotiated by ministry personnel in order to move forward. Bureaucracy is not usually created to control (though sometimes it is) but rather to ensure that right decisions are made and right directions pursued. However, boards that require all decisions to come to them, leaders who demand the same from team members, and organizations that build layers of oversight often create unhealthy and unnecessary forms of bureaucracy.

In the absence of a sandbox-like mechanism to give direction, it is not surprising that bureaucracy develops. It is a management mechanism (awkward as it is) that keeps people and ministries on track. Again, leaders play a significant role in whether bureaucracy is part of their culture. Healthy organizations operate with the fewest layers of management possible.

3. The dysfunction of ambiguity. Ambiguity is ubiquitous in ministry organizations. Often the mission is so broad it cannot be quantified. The values are so general they cannot define the ministry and affect day-to-day activities. Most ministries have never identified the central ministry focus they must concentrate on day in and day out. And it is rare to find a ministry that has thoughtfully articulated the preferred culture they are committed to create.

Ambiguity about these core issues makes it very difficult to achieve any kind of significant organizational alignment—one does not have anything with which to align! It also means team members can claim to be in alignment whether or not they are. And team members find it difficult to know how to make good decisions or focus efforts.

On the other hand, it is deeply refreshing to find organizations that are crystal clear about who they are, where they are going, what their central ministry focus is, and what kind of culture they are creating. Where you find this clarity, you also find highly motivated and focused team members who have great personal clarity.

I have worked in the national office of the EFCA for twenty years. It is a great organization. However, for the first eight or so years we had a very nebulous idea of our mission. Apart from running good programs and focusing on church planting, it was hard to define what we were about apart from being a "denominational office." Then we made a major transition as we worked through a process to define a new mission statement: "The EFCA exists to glorify God by multiplying healthy churches among all people." Suddenly we had meaningful targets that were not simply about numbers. We were about multiplication of churches, the health of churches, becoming a movement of "all people" in the United States, and reaching "all people" globally. These four foci began to drive everything we did. At the same time, we determined we needed to be a service organization for our churches. By helping them become all they could be (the local church is God's chosen instrument to reach the world) we fulfilled our mandate.

Today, our surveys show that about 98 percent of our pastors know and believe in EFCA's mission. And because our churches voluntarily send financial donations to the national office, they vote on our effectiveness with their pocketbooks. In the past decade, financial support has increased dramatically. All this is the result of moving from ambiguity to clarity and then living out that clarity.

4. The dysfunction of professional ministry. The fourth dysfunction applies particularly to churches and mission organizations. It is the thinking that only those with formal training are able to minister effectively. If you doubt this is true in your denomination, just try to name pastors without formal theological training — can one even be ordained without it? In the local church, this dysfunction also shows itself when lay people are not given significant ministry responsibility and full-time personnel don't make a concerted effort to release others into ministry.

Here is something to chew on: There is no intrinsic link between one's level of formal education and one's ministry effectiveness! Educators may want you to believe there is, but there isn't. I am amazed at those, for instance, who receive a PhD in Organizational Leadership but cannot lead anything. Because my work is international, I know hundreds of pastors leading highly effective ministries who have never had formal theological education. Often, they have not even been educated beyond the secondary level (what *does* matter is that pastors have a level of education consistent with those in their congregation). For those without formal theological education, ongoing training through a nonformal means is critical.

I'm not antieducation (I hold an MDiv from a great seminary). What troubles me is the culture we have bred that leaves highly qualified people out of the game because they lack a degree. In fact, when churches are looking for staff members, the first place I suggest they look is inside their congregations to identify spiritually mature people with the appropriate skill sets. Leaders know those people, the people know the churches, and leaders know whether the match will be good based on long experience—rather than hoping that someone called from the outside will be a fit.

A special plea to pastors. Pastors can fall prey to a particular form of the dysfunction of professional ministry: believing that they must personally fulfill all the roles their position seems to demand. If you are a pastor, the requirement that you must lead is usually nonnegotiable. But, let's face it, many of us are not wired very significantly in the leadership area—that's not what we signed up in ministry to do.

God never asked us to be what we cannot be. All of us are gifted in a few specific areas, and everything else is a weakness. If leadership is not our primary gift, we are fooling ourselves that we can be the prime mover. Our weaknesses will never be our strengths. We need to bring around us a team of qualified individuals who can play to strengths we do not have so that we can use strengths we do have.

The most untapped resources in our churches are lay people who could use their leadership skills to come alongside pastors and, as a team, bring a level of leadership to the congregation that would infuse it with huge energy, creativity, and missional impact. When we don't tap into those resources we leave a massive resource unused on the table. Yet, surrounded by people who could help us, we refuse to share the leadership ministry in any substantive way, fail to seek their counsel, and neglect to invite them to help us lead more effectively. One day God might ask us why.

What gets in the way of this happening? First is our assumption that the pastor must be the leader. Certainly pastors must be primary spokespersons for vision, but why would they expect they must be primary developers of mission, vision, and strategy if that is not their gift? It is theologically contradictory. Second, I think it is an ego issue. We look at great leaders who pastor large churches and think we should be able to do that. Our egos get in the way of realizing that their gifts are not our gifts. We forget that the mission and effectiveness of our congregations is more important than our egos and that we need help.

I am an advocate of finding the best possible people and asking them to serve on the senior leadership board of the church. Then we should invite the best of *those* leaders to help craft the most missionally compelling ministry paradigm the church could possibly have. Ministry is not about us—it is about Jesus and His kingdom, bringing the maximum number of people to Him, and deploying them in meaningful ministry so that we reach maturity in Christ (see Ephesians 4).

The alternative to this biblical view of gifts and to the humility that admits we need help? The ineffectiveness of so many churches. Bob is an example. He is the quintessential shepherd/pastor: high relational skills and great caring skills. His preaching skills were good enough that the church he led grew to about five hundred. Each time it reached that level, though, it was as if it hit a ceiling; attendance would level off for a while and then decrease.

The church was filled with highly trained professionals, many with strong leadership gifts; several led large organizations. Over time, Bob invited many of these people on to the board. Once there, however, they experienced huge frustration because they were not invited to help lead the church in any strategic way. That was Bob's prerogative; he saw himself at their level and could not admit he needed help (and these were friends who desperately wanted to help him).

When a crisis developed over the lack of congregational direction and people started to migrate out of the church (lack of missional direction will do that), Bob clung to the belief that he was a leader and could solve the problem. He could not and eventually resigned, bitter and angry, under the pressure of a church in leadership crisis. Six months later he found another congregation where the scenario played itself out again; two years later he was asked to leave over failed leadership.

Bob and the two congregations could have been saved a whole lot of pain if he had admitted that missional and directional leadership were not his strong suits. He could have surrounded himself with willing leaders who would have played to their strengths while he played to his, and together they could have led the congregations to places of missional effectiveness. But his ego would not let him do this, and the churches suffered because of it.

I think it would be fair to say that God wired me to lead. Yet I have a leadership team that includes ten other great leaders who complement me in areas where I do not have strengths. Some of these people have formal theological education; some do not. All are leaders; all are mature Christ followers. Without this team, ReachGlobal would not be what it is today. Most pastors will not have that kind of leadership capital on their senior staff team, but they probably have people in their church who are waiting to be tapped to help lead.

H. I. BEST PRACTICE

Healthy pastors don't pretend to be something they are not. They learn to lead the best they can and surround themselves with qualified leaders for the sake of the church's ministry and the kingdom of God. Healthy pastors are not ego-driven. They are missionally driven and desire to bring the best people to the table so the church can be everything God wants it to be.

H. I. MOMENT

How much leadership capital have you left on the table because you have not tapped into leadership gifting within your congregation or organization?

5. The dysfunction of mistrust. Mistrust hurts the organization, hurts productivity (people who don't trust one another don't work well together), contributes to silos (lack of synergy keeps us to ourselves), and ultimately detracts from our return on mission.

Mistrust is often the child of two dysfunctions we've considered: control and bureaucracy. At its core, control comes from not trusting others to make healthy and wise decisions. Control and mistrust are two sides of the same coin. If we cannot trust teams to make good decisions, we have either hired/retained the wrong people or have not been clear enough on who we are and where we are going.

Mistrust flourishes when there is not proper clarity, when boundaries are not defined (how do I know what I can and cannot do?), when communication is lacking (the more I know the more I can trust), when one must secure permission at many levels (why don't they let me make the decision?), and when healthy relationships have not been established (I can't trust you when I don't know you). Mistrust also flourishes when leaders don't live by the same standards and commitments that they ask their teams to live by.

There is a growing recognition in the secular world that trust is a core issue organizations must deal with if they desire to be healthy. Patrick Lencioni sees mistrust as the central core issue of team dysfunction in his compelling book *Overcoming the Five Dysfunctions of a Team*. Stephen Covey has written a significant book on organizational trust, *The Speed of Trust: The One Thing That Changes Everything*. Trust matters!

Trust ought to be most prevalent in Christian organizations where the culture of Christ should be more pervasive than the culture of our world. This is an elephant that must be confronted if a ministry or team is going to be healthy.

PRACTICES THAT CONTRIBUTE TO A CULTURE OF MISTRUST

Because trust among teams is so important, we will go into the causes and antidotes of mistrust in more depth. The following practices help create a culture of mistrust.

Approaching others from the outset with an attitude of mistrust. An unfortunate and often pervasive attitude in the church and Christian organizations is a built-in mistrust of anyone who is in leadership. This attitude says, "I will not trust you until you prove that I can" (the reverse of how a healthy individual thinks). Rather than making the role of leaders a joy (see Hebrews 13:17), leading becomes a burden because leaders are constantly fighting against this damaging culture.

Assuming poor motives. This attitude believes, "Everyone is going to let us down or make decisions we would not make." Unfortunately, many of us quickly default to a position of mistrust—assuming bad motives behind an action or decision. Invariably, when I have made that assumption, I've failed to find bad motives when I clarified the situation. There may have been poor judgment, or issues and circumstances I was not aware of, but the motives were not bad.

Believing something to be true when one does not have the facts. Leaders often find out months or even years after making a decision that people in the organization deeply distrust them because they assumed certain (untrue) information about the situation.

Taking on someone else's offense. Mistrust can build when an individual takes on another's offense, usually without knowing all the facts. Healthy individuals understand there is more than one side to a story and do not draw conclusions without doing due diligence.

BUILDING TRUST

Healthy individuals and teams practice three commitments that directly contribute to a culture of trust:

1. I will choose to trust you unless you give me a reason not to.
2. I will assume your motives are right even when I disagree with you.
3. I will be proactive in clarifying issues rather than assuming something to be true.

In addition, the following practices help create a trusting environment when teams adopt them.

TRUST BUSTERS AND TRUST BUILDERS

Trust Buster: Starting from mistrust
Trust Builder: Choosing to trust
You can count on me to trust you unless you give me a reason not to do so. In the event that trust is broken, I will clarify how trust can be reestablished. I will always start from a position of trust rather than a position of mistrust.

Trust Buster: Being vague and fuzzy

Trust Builder: Being candid and up-front

You can count on me to tell you what I am thinking, what my expectations are, how I perceive your strengths and weaknesses, and, if there is a performance issue, what you need to do to solve it. You may not always agree with me, but you can count on me to be clear about what I am thinking and why.

Trust Buster: Breaking my promises

Trust Builder: Keeping my promises

I will commit to those things that I can commit to, and you can count on me to follow through. If for some reason I find myself unable to keep a promise, I will tell you. I will not commit to those things that I know I cannot deliver on.

Trust Buster: Acting inconsistently

Trust Builder: Acting consistently

My life will match my words, and you can count on me to be consistent in how I treat those who report to me, in the pattern of my life, and in living out the commitments of the organization. Inconsistency will be an exception rather than the rule.

Trust Buster: Not engaging in real dialogue

Trust Builder: Listening carefully

I will listen to and dialogue with you respectfully and will be candid in my responses. This means there is always opportunity for dialogue, questions, and clarification. My commitment is to consider your opinions and suggestions carefully even if I choose a different path in the end.

Trust Buster: Giving preferential treatment

Trust Builder: Being fair and equitable

You can expect me to act with your best interests in mind and to seek always to be fair and equitable in decisions that affect you.

Trust Buster: Using people

Trust Builder: Caring for people

You can expect me to care about you genuinely as a whole person and never simply use you for my or the organization's purposes. This means I will also seek to engage you in your sweet spot — that place where there is convergence between your gifts and our needs.

Trust Buster: Being secretive or impossible to "read"
Trust Builder: Being self-disclosing
You can expect me to be appropriately self-disclosing about who I am, what I am thinking, where I am going, and my own challenges.

Trust Buster: Controlling
Trust Builder: Empowering
Where you are given responsibility I will empower you to carry it out within clearly articulated boundaries rather than micromanaging or controlling you.

Trust Buster: Making assumptions
Trust Builder: Clarifying
If it appears you have violated my trust or acted inappropriately, I will ask you for clarification rather than assuming you deliberately chose to do something unwise or inappropriate.

Many relationships in our world are based on mistrust rather than trust, and we bring these biases into our ministries. Yet, in God's economy, there ought to be a high level of trust unless there is reason to think otherwise. Leaders develop cultures of either trust or mistrust.

Leaders must constantly address trust with their teams. I make it a point to monitor trust levels among my senior team. Where I think there is slippage, I will find ways to address it because trust is key to our success in working together.

Members of healthy teams choose to trust one another. High-impact leaders ensure trust is fostered by good communication, clear expectations and boundaries, elimination of unnecessary tollbooths, and accountability within clearly defined limits.

BE PROACTIVE IN DEVELOPING A HEALTHY CULTURE

After looking at the dysfunctions of many cultures, it should be obvious that culture cannot be ignored without significant cost. The development of a healthy culture is central to getting the missional results one desires. The good news is that you do not need to settle for the culture

you have but can proactively define the culture you want to develop and systematically move in that direction.

Wanting to change culture is not about dishonoring the past. Times, circumstances, opportunities, and organizations change. In fact, organizations that remain static are headed for history themselves. We honor the past but reenvision for the future — taking today's realities and opportunities into account.

Pastor Steven Goold pastors a large suburban church in New Hope, Minnesota, with a rich history of effective ministry. For most of its history the church was defined by its white, upper middle-class congregation. Over the past decade, something dramatic happened. The surrounding community evolved into a diverse, multiethnic neighborhood.

After much prayer, discussion, and planning, Steve and his leaders embarked on a difficult, rewarding, risky venture. They set out to transition the church's culture to embrace the less affluent, multiethnic nature of the community. They were convinced their church needed to reflect their neighborhood even if that meant radical changes in practices and culture.

Think of the difference in culture between an upper middle-class, predominantly white ministry and that of a multiethnic, less affluent ministry. Such a transition required huge resolve because, as you can imagine, not everyone was enamored with the need to change. But a commitment to honor God in new circumstances that required a new culture be crafted.

The past was honored and treasured in the transition. The rich history of Crystal Evangelical Free Church is the foundation upon which a new ministry and culture is being built as New Hope Church (the name was changed to reflect the name of their city).

Steve and his leaders understand what many others do not: In different seasons, God gives ministries opportunities that require different responses. In the process, they set out on a journey of cultural transformation that will affect everything they do.

H. I. MOMENT

Jot down some descriptors of the culture you would like for your organization. Then write a one-sentence definition of that culture. Remember that organizational culture is the unspoken ethos of a group of people, including its beliefs, social behaviors, practices, attitudes, values, and traditions — all of which contribute to a collective mode of thinking and acting.

_____

_____

_____

_____

_____

If you think back to the sandbox defined by ReachGlobal, you will realize that the four sides describe not only our ministry philosophy but also the culture we are intentionally creating.

As a mission that sent its first missionaries in 1887, ReachGlobal operated very much in the black-and-white world in which it began. Like Crystal Evangelical Free Church, ReachGlobal was at a critical junction and needed to change in order to best meet the needs of missions in a globalized world. So, using the sandbox picture, we set out several years ago on a five- to seven-year culture change. As part of that process, we changed our name to ReachGlobal. Principles like teams, partnerships, empowerment, and entrepreneurial spirit were significant transformations to our culture.

Changing culture has major ramifications. For ReachGlobal, it meant changes in how decisions are made (they are driven down to the lowest possible level), how intentionally we live (all personnel have KRAs and AMPs), how we do leadership (we have transitioned from a culture where leaders are administrators to a culture where leaders lead), how we work together (in teams, not as lone rangers), how we partner with nationals (we serve them and their movements), how we view alignment (it is now around the sandbox, not around methodology), and how we view health (health affects our organization at every level: individuals, teams, leaders, and churches).

REALITIES OF CHANGING A CULTURE

ReachGlobal and New Hope Church have experienced a core reality of culture change: It will be a process over time. Since most people naturally resist change, the gravitational pull back to the old norm will often be huge—and powerful.

Beware of believing that true cultural change has taken place when superficial behavioral changes are made (people will do what they need to do even if they don't believe in the change). I am sure there are a few in my own organization who are thinking to themselves, *We'll wait it out, and things will go back to the way they were, like they always do.* They are not bad people, just change-resistant people who like the old way (it's their culture).

I am convinced that true cultural change takes five to ten years and is proven when the new thinking, attitudes, and methodology become the norm rather than the exception. This is why pastors who bring spiritual renovation to their churches face such stiff opposition. They are fighting the prevailing culture.

If one is intent on significant cultural change, it is often necessary to bring in new leaders who have not been part of the old culture and therefore find it easy to embrace the new. This will cause anxiety (as all change does), but these new leaders do not have to deal with the old baggage.

Be absolutely sure your senior teams (in my case, the president of the denomination and the ReachGlobal board, along with the senior team I lead) buy into the culture you are seeking to create. If you are a pastor, this means your board. Their participation in the process is important because they will be your key supporters once you roll out the new cultural paradigm. The natural inertia of the organization will seek to bring you back to "normal," so support at the highest level is key to successful cultural transformation.

Your next challenge is the team you personally lead. Ultimately, every team member must embrace the culture you are seeking to create, or they need to be shifted or replaced. You will not be able to identify these needs immediately. Some people will give intellectual assent to a new model but are incapable of embracing it at a deep level, even if they want to. Some just won't get it. Some may not agree with it. But you cannot have senior staff members who sabotage the new model (directly or passively). If the change is substantial, it may take you twelve to fifteen months to ascertain where people stand.

SENIOR LEADERS ARE THE CHAMPIONS OF THE CULTURE

We said in the prior chapter that the core job of the senior leader is to bring clarity to the organization about who they are, what their mission is, where they are going, and how they are going to get there. Consistency of the senior leader's message over time becomes a key factor in creating a new culture within an organization. While senior leaders do many other things, if they do not do this, they have failed as leaders.

A carefully constructed sandbox is a powerful tool for helping people understand those four areas. My first priority is to help my organization understand the sandbox and its implications. People may not even understand that what I am describing is a new culture, which is fine. What matters is that they start to understand, embrace, and practice what the sandbox describes. If I ever tire of being the evangelist for the sandbox and what it represents, it is time for me to turn the reins over to someone else, because without a clearly articulated culture embraced by the majority, we will never be all that God has called us to be.

I do this not only in presentations but also through dialogue in groups, one on one, and by e-mail (I answer every e-mail I receive from our staff). It takes time for people to grasp implications, deal with their anxiety, and figure out what the new culture means for them. Helping them do this is part of the leader's job.

At times, when I receive significant pushback or skepticism, I answer, "Do not underestimate my resolve." I want our personnel to understand that the changes are not going away, that we will overcome whatever obstacles we need to overcome, and that we are absolutely committed to living the implications of the sandbox. That knowledge, by the way, is very helpful for people who wonder if this is a fad or if leaders are really serious. Leaders who easily change direction engender skepticism rather than trust. Many people are more concerned with consistency and clarity than with the specifics of the direction.

Leaders themselves must be very clear about the organization's direction, believe in it, and act according to it. When people bounce ideas off me and want to know my opinion, my routine response is, "How does it fit the sandbox?" Once they can articulate how it fits the sandbox, I am glad to have a conversation about the merits of the idea.

I remember the day one of our leaders in ReachGlobal was talking to me about a couple on the field who were not healthy and needed some help if they were going to be effective long-term. "Why don't you tell them that they cannot come back to the field until they have received help for the issue you are concerned about," I said.

"You mean I can do that?" he said.

"Of course you can," I replied. "It is the fourth side of the sandbox—healthy people."

"Oh," he said. "I didn't know we could actually deal with it."

I had to smile internally. When leaders always refer decisions back to the principles of the sandbox and insist that the culture being created reflects the sandbox, people start to get the idea that the organization is serious about the culture it has said it believes in.

LEADERS LIVE THE SANDBOX

As a leader, I never want to violate the culture we are trying to create, and I want to model what it means to live consistently with our commitments.

One of our commitments is that we believe in teams and lead through teams. That means I also lead through a team and do not make unilateral decisions on issues that should be vetted through my team. If I honor this commitment, my team members will be likely to do the same with their teams in turn.

Because our central ministry focus (side three of the sandbox) is to develop, empower, and release healthy personnel and national leaders, my time and energies must reflect that. Thus I spend a major part of my time equipping and training leaders. The example I set in living out our core focus sends a powerful message to our leaders as to what we expect them to do.

One of our guiding principles is that we do multiplication rather than addition. This means we are always looking for ways to multiply the impact of ministry for the greatest kingdom leverage. The very writing of this book is an indication of my commitment to do multiplication. What would happen if every key ministry player in every church and organization were required to train one or two others to do their jobs? All of a sudden, a church with a staff of five would actually have a "staff" of ten or fifteen. That almost sounds like what Ephesians 4:12 is talking about!

Leaders who live their sandbox demonstrate their deep resolve that the culture of the sandbox becomes the culture of the organization. By insisting that all of their senior leaders live the sandbox, that demonstration starts to go deep. Pretty soon it is evident to everyone that "this is our culture."

We indicated earlier that one of the five dysfunctions of the church is ambiguity. Do not underestimate the power of clarity and the ability to be very defining. That is the power of the sandbox when leaders live it and call their teams to live it as well.

USE YOUR SANDBOX TO DEFINE AND DRIVE CULTURE

It is liberating to realize we can intentionally define the culture we want to create for our ministries—whether they are parachurch or the local church. You have already taken a stab at identifying the kind of culture your ministry currently has as well as the culture you would like.

In the next chapter, you will have the opportunity to build that preferred culture through your own sandbox. In the meantime, keep thinking about your preferred culture and its ramifications for the values and guiding principles you adopt.

Ignoring culture inevitably puts an organization on a slide toward decline. Using culture change as leverage to lead the organization toward healthy and effective ministry in today's and tomorrow's environment can be a powerful accelerator for healthy and effective ministry.

Remember that every organization has a culture. It is either an accidental culture or one intentionally designed to achieve maximum ministry results in a healthy way. The culture is a combination of the four sides of your sandbox. Too many leaders spend far too little time creating, defining, and championing a culture that will help their organizations become all they can be. Those who do, achieve far more than those who don't, and they elicit great loyalty from their staff. Anyone who leads at any level is responsible for his or her group's culture. Good leaders create healthy and effective cultures — intentionally.

H. I. QUESTIONS FOR TEAM DISCUSSION

Which of the five common dysfunctions of ministry organizations does your organization suffer from?

How did you define your current organizational culture?

How did you define your preferred culture?

How does your present culture either help or hinder the ministry of your organization?

CHAPTER FOUR

BUILDING YOUR SANDBOX

CHAPTER SUMMARY:

The sandbox helps you visualize and communicate the most important aspects of your organization. The process of "building" your
sandbox involves defining the ministry philosophy and culture you
are intentionally creating. The sandbox brings clarity, in a single
picture, to the complexity of your organization. The sandbox asks
you to consider four sides:

1. The *mission* side represents the reason for your existence. It
   clarifies what you want to accomplish.
2. The *guiding-principles* side defines the core commitments you
   want everyone to live by and clarifies those things that are
   nonnegotiable.
3. The *central-ministry-focus* side answers the question, "What is
   the most important thing we must do, day in and day out, to
   fulfill our mission?"
4. The *preferred-culture* side is the culture you must create if you
   are going to realize the potential of your organization and
   accomplish your mission.

The sandbox becomes your key clarifying tool for leaders, volunteers, and members of your organization. The goal is for everyone

to use his or her gifts and wiring in creative ways for the kingdom of God, but to stay inside the sandbox.

Maximum clarity is a priority for every organization; building your sandbox forces you to articulate mission, guiding principles, central ministry focus, and preferred culture. Without definition on these issues, an organization is doomed to mediocrity—something none of us desire.

I cannot stress enough the importance of being able to visualize the key components of your ministry in one picture. As a leader, you may be able to keep those important elements in your mind at all times. Most others cannot and will not. The sandbox reminds everyone of the four most important aspects of the organization at one glance. There are no stashed-away values or lost mission statements or unclear cultural ideals. They are all there in a unified whole with the constant reminder that all four sides matter and that we are all responsible to play inside that particular sandbox. Remember, "out of sight, out of mind"—which is the reality in most organizations!

Before we look at examples of real-life sandboxes, let's consider how you might begin to articulate the elements of the four sides for your church or organization. Whether you choose to use the sandbox picture or some other tool, you must come to clarity in these four areas to be successful in the long-term.

Because the sandbox terminology is clear in the United States but may not be applicable elsewhere, various other metaphors are used internationally. Some use a soccer field, some a "ministry table." One Baptist church in the United States uses an altar as the metaphor. The goal is to find a metaphor that is understandable in the culture you work in and that clarifies in picture form the most critical elements of mission, guiding principles, central ministry focus, and preferred culture.

SIDE ONE: MISSION

Your mission represents your "true north"—the reason for your existence. Mission statements should be specific enough to be clear but broad enough that they are rarely fulfilled. Mission statements do not define how an organization meets the mission but clarify what the organization exists to accomplish. Here are examples of good mission statements:

- "The mission of the EFCA is to glorify God by multiplying healthy churches among all people."
- "The mission of Rockpoint Church is to guide people into a life-changing relationship with Jesus Christ."
- "The mission of Life International is to multiply life-giving ministries wherever abortion exists around the world."

Each of these statements presents a clear definition of why the organization exists. Whether you are developing a new mission statement or evaluating a current one, the following principles from *High-Impact Church Boards* will be helpful in your process.

Make it simple and clear. If your mission statement requires a paragraph of explanation, it's too complex. As you develop your mission statement, give it sufficient time to percolate among leaders so you can refine, simplify, and clarify.

Be specific. The more general your statement, the less helpful it will be. For instance, "The mission of Christ Church is to bring glory to God" is theologically correct but so nonspecific it is of little use as a directional tool. On the other hand, "The mission of Christ Church is to bring God glory by lovingly introducing people to Jesus and helping them grow in Him" is far more focused. It includes elements (evangelism, spiritual growth, and a climate of love) that can be measured.

Be sure it's yours. Be wary of adopting someone else's mission statement. Allow God to be creative through *your* leadership to develop a statement that is true to your context.

Ask, "Can I get excited about the mission?" Leaders need to embrace the mission with passion and rigorous resolve. Passion comes from believing this is the mission for *your* organization, something you as a leader are willing to follow long-term.

SIDE TWO: GUIDING PRINCIPLES, OR VALUES

I liken guiding principles to the channel markers one encounters when piloting a boat in inland waterways. The green and red buoys are there for one reason: to keep you and your boat out of danger. They tell you that as long as you stay inside the channel, you are in safe water. It amazes me how many pilots think they don't need to stay inside the channel—and find out the hard way that shallow water or shoals are not good for their boats' hulls!

In the same way, an organization's guiding principles clearly delineate the channel everyone is to stay within. If you review ReachGlobal's guiding principles (pages 36–38), you will see they provide concrete guidance to all personnel about how they must approach their work. Many organizations have values that are so general they provide no real guidance and are therefore ignored. I asked the president of an organization this week what his organization's guiding principles were, and he could not even remember them. Obviously they were of no help to him or others.

Guiding principles serve several purposes central to a healthy organization. First, they allow you to define the core commitments you want everyone to live by. For instance, "team" is a nonnegotiable commitment in our organization. Our guiding principle of "team led and team driven" makes it clear that everyone works in a team context.

Second, guiding principles allow you to craft the kind of ministry values and commitments you want to permeate your organization. When all your personnel live by the same set of values, you start to get significant alignment.

Third, guiding principles clarify those things that are nonnegotiable. By doing so, you prevent the unintended consequences of traveling outside the channel markers.

Finally, a well-chosen set of guiding principles gives your organization permission to choose certain courses of action. One of our guiding principles is that "we measure results." That sends a strong message that everyone must be productive versus simply busy. One of the guiding principles of a church I know is, "We are multigenerational." They are committed to meeting the spiritual needs of all generations. On the one hand, this means they cannot exclude age groups when making ministry decisions. On the other hand, it means they can design special ministries to meet special needs. It guides and gives permission for ministry choices.

To get to clarity on guiding principles, you can ask these questions:

- What are the nonnegotiables that apply to our whole organization?
- Around what things must we have absolute alignment by everyone on the team?
- What principles, if followed, will keep our organization in safe waters?
- If we had to describe the most important principles of how we do what we do, what would they be?

To be meaningful, guiding principles should include an explanation of what the principle means in your organization. That way they can truly guide behavior.

Well-written guiding principles not only are the channel markers for the ministry, but they also empower personnel to make decisions consistent with the principles. They provide both empowerment and accountability.

SIDE THREE: CENTRAL MINISTRY FOCUS

Your organization's central ministry focus answers the question, "What is the most important thing we must do, day in and day out, to best fulfill our mission?" This question is not always easy to answer, but it is critical.

For the church, I believe the answer focuses on Ephesians 4 and the developing, empowering, and releasing of people into meaningful ministry in line with their God-given gifting. Making that the central ministry focus in churches would considerably change the impact of the local church. One church defined their central ministry focus as that of helping people take the next step in their spiritual growth, a concept in sync with Ephesians 4:12.

For ReachGlobal, the answer focuses on developing, empowering, and releasing our personnel and national leaders. We multiply ourselves through others.

The central ministry focus does not identify the *only* way to accomplish one's mission. It should, however, be the most *effective* and leveraged means to see maximum ministry results. In ReachGlobal, one way to reach our mission would be to have our missionaries personally plant churches. However, by focusing on developing, empowering, and releasing healthy national leaders, we can see a quantum increase in the quality and quantity of healthy churches planted. If we stay true to our central ministry focus, we will see more ministry results than we would from anything else we could do.

To get to your central ministry focus, ask these questions:

- What is the single most important thing we could do that would give us the most leverage in accomplishing our mission?
- If there was one practice everyone in the organization needed to pay attention to, what would it be?
- If we want to see maximum ministry impact in line with our mission, what is the one thing we must do on a regular basis?

If you get the answers to these questions right, and if over a period of years you insist everyone pay attention to and live the central ministry focus, your organization will start to see return on mission like it has never seen before.

SIDE FOUR: PREFERRED CULTURE

The fourth side of the sandbox is the preferred culture you are committed to creating that will maximize your ministry's impact and achieve your missional goals. At ReachGlobal this has to do with a culture of health: healthy personnel, teams, leaders, and churches. We made health in these four areas our desired culture, knowing we would never accomplish our mission without these areas of health. We also knew that with health here, we have the best chance of fulfilling our mission.

For the local church, I believe this side of the sandbox has to do with a culture of spiritual transformation or vitality, however one chooses to describe that. Without spiritual transformation where the hearts, minds, relationships, and priorities of individuals are transformed into what Christ wants for us, there will be no fruit or ministry impact. In *High-Impact Ministry Boards*, I recommend leaders define what a healthy or mature Christ follower looks like. That way, you are able to design your teaching to help individuals reach the goal of spiritual maturity, and thus bring corporate health as well. If you can identify five to eight characteristics of a spiritually vital Christ follower, this becomes your church's fourth side of the sandbox. It also becomes the target each ministry within the church pays close attention to so all ministries move individuals toward maturity.

It is important to remember we are not after a set of behaviors when we talk about spiritual transformation. We can convince people to exhibit certain behaviors without true life transformation. It is a change of heart, mind, relationships, and priorities that transforms thinking and behaviors. However it is defined, it seems to me that the desired culture of the ministries in our churches is that of individual life transformation that then exhibits itself through changed thinking, relationships, hearts, and life priorities.

It is my conviction that the book of Ephesians is a key element for any discussion regarding church desired culture—and therefore the development of a church sandbox. This short book gives all four sides of the sandbox significant attention; it is the seminal New Testament book on healthy churches.

Whatever type of organization you have, your desired culture needs to be thought through very carefully because it is what makes possible the realization of your mission. For instance, the definition of success in many mission organizations for years was how many personnel they had and how many countries they were in. That led them to accept staff who were not healthy (and caused major problems for those they worked with) and to enter new fields without adequate staff or infrastructure. Thus, while the definition made sense, it was actually a definition of success that brought negative consequences.

The definition of your desired culture has three major implications. First, you have a way to measure success in your ministry. Second, it forces you to grapple with what your desired culture really is. Third, it gives your staff the target they are working toward and alignment around that target. Most organizations have not thought deeply about what they really want to accomplish, except in general terms that are not very measurable.

Once defined, the sandbox becomes the culture we desire our organizations to reflect, and it becomes a teaching tool for staff, volunteers, and congregations.

EXAMPLES OF LOCAL-CHURCH SANDBOXES

Following are examples of sandboxes adopted by local churches. In the diagrams, you can see how the churches used the sandbox picture itself as the summary of the four elements. Then you'll see how the second church, Rockpoint, fleshed out their sandbox elements in writing.

Bridgeport Bible Fellowship Church
Bridgeport, Connecticut

Love God, Love People
We exist to share the love of Christ

We believe every believer should be committed to:

- Spiritual growth
- Worship
- Submission to Christ
- The mission of Christ
- The Word of God
- Fellowship and relationship with one another
- Community
- Service

MISSION

PREFERRED CULTURE

GUIDING PRINCIPLES

Creativity
Humility
Resolve
Interdependence
Simplicity
Transformation

CENTRAL MINISTRY FOCUS

Sharing the love of Christ through outreach and discipleship ministries

Grace Baptist Church
Santa Clarita, California

We exist to make and multiply Christ followers
who magnify the glory of God

Our goals for Christ followers:
- Love from pure hearts
- Good consciences
- Authentic faith

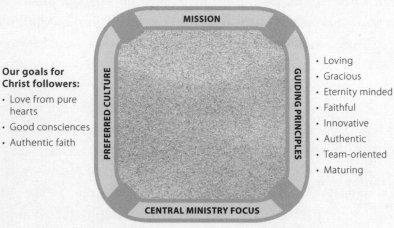

- Loving
- Gracious
- Eternity minded
- Faithful
- Innovative
- Authentic
- Team-oriented
- Maturing

To accomplish our mission we must teach and model God's Word in the power
of the Spirit, engaging our world as agents of change

Rockpoint Church
Lake Elmo, Minnesota

We exist to guide people into a life-changing
relationship with Jesus Christ

- Grace
- Growth
- Gifts
- Generosity
- Gathering

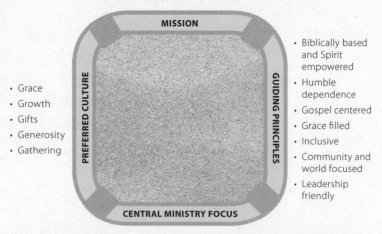

- Biblically based and Spirit empowered
- Humble dependence
- Gospel centered
- Grace filled
- Inclusive
- Community and world focused
- Leadership friendly

To encourage and facilitate everyone to actively use their abilities, skills, and
spiritual gifts in service to Christ and the advancement of His gospel
(Ephesians 4:11-16)

ROCKPOINT CHURCH MINISTRY SANDBOX

Side One: Mission
We exist to guide people into a life-changing relationship with Jesus Christ.

Side Two: Guiding Principles
Biblically based and Spirit empowered. The Scriptures are the Word of God and the guide for our lives. We neither add to nor detract from His Word in our teaching. The Spirit of God gives us the empowerment needed for living lives that are pleasing to God. It is the dual ministry of the Word and Spirit that gives us the ability to follow Jesus and bring spiritual transformation to our lives.

Humble dependence. We recognize that we can do nothing of lasting spiritual impact without the power of the Holy Spirit. Jesus said, "Apart from me you can do nothing" of eternal significance, but if we remain in Him we will "bear much fruit" (John 15:5). We are therefore committed to humble dependence on God in each of our ministries through concerted prayer, staying close to Christ, and recognizing that all we do is for Him.

Gospel centered. The heart of the gospel is that Jesus came to die for our sins, redeem us, transform us into His image, and give us eternal life. All of our ministries are designed to help people experience the joy of becoming one of God's children, experience the daily presence of Christ, and follow Him more closely. We are committed to seeing authentic life transformation through the Holy Spirit, who empowers us to live out the gospel in service to Christ rather than conformity to our world.

Grace filled. We are a community that practices the example of Jesus in showing grace to one another and to those who do not know Jesus. This includes forgiving one another when an offense has been committed, avoiding legalism in all of its forms, loving one another unconditionally, and honoring individual choices in areas where Scripture is silent. We are committed to treating one another with love and respect and to following the biblical guidelines for conflict resolution.

Inclusive. All people matter to God and are of equal value in His sight. We welcome all who desire to find and follow Christ. We are committed to ministries that meet the needs of all generations and to go out of our way, like Jesus, to love and minister to those who are hurting, needy, or marginalized by society.

Community and world focused. We have a deep commitment to bring the good news of Christ to our community and world through evangelism and ministries of compassion. We are committed to showing the love of Christ by meeting needs within our community. Rockpoint is outward looking in its focus and desires to be a voice of hope and help to those around us. Ministries of compassion are close to the heart of God and a priority for Rockpoint.

Leadership friendly. We believe that God designed the church to be led by a leadership board of godly individuals who will ensure the spiritual health, ministry direction, and intentionality of the staff and congregation. We are committed to strong leadership working in team toward this end. We believe that healthy team ministry at all levels, working under the leadership board, will directly impact the effectiveness of our ministries.

Side Three: Central Ministry Focus

The central ministry focus of Rockpoint is to encourage and facilitate everyone to actively use their abilities, skills, and spiritual gifts in service to Christ and the advancement of His gospel (Ephesians 4:11-16).

Side Four: Preferred Culture

We are committed to a culture of spiritual vitality at Rockpoint Church. This means that our lives should be characterized by the following priorities that flow from the love of God and that define one who is following Christ closely.

Grace. God's grace in our lives is undeserved and cannot be earned. It is a free gift from a loving God, who has redeemed us. We accept His grace with thanksgiving, live in His grace through the power of the Holy Spirit, and share that grace with others through loving relationships, acts of service, and the concern of Christ toward others.

Growth. The Christian life is one of ongoing growth into the character of Christ. We are committed to a culture that facilitates real life change rather than settling for a mere intellectual faith. We believe that keys to life change include the practice of prayer, time in the Word, and fellowship with others, as well as a commitment to personal obedience to Christ.

Gifts. Our lives are incomplete unless we are actively using our gifts and talents to serve others and advance the cause of Christ. We strongly encourage every believer to be actively involved in ministry in line with their gifting on a regular basis in the church and in their sphere of influence. We will only be fully healthy as a congregation when all are using their varied gifts that together complement and complete one another.

Generosity. Just as Christ freely gave His life for us, He calls us to generously share what God has entrusted to us for the advancement of His gospel. We take seriously the words of Jesus, "Where your treasure is, there your heart will be also" (Matthew 6:21). We are called to be a people who are stewards of God's resources, freely give back to Christ a portion of what He has given us, and care for the needs of others in the body.

Gathering. The Scriptures tell us that we are to live in community with others within our church, love one another, care for one another, carry one another's burdens, and encourage one another. We were not designed to live in isolation but to grow, live, and minister in a loving, caring community.

EXAMPLES OF AN ORGANIZATIONAL SANDBOX

You were introduced to the ReachGlobal sandbox in chapter 2. I've included it again here so you can see an organization's sandbox in contrast with the church sandboxes. I'm also using a sandbox from Life International for another example.

ReachGlobal Sandbox

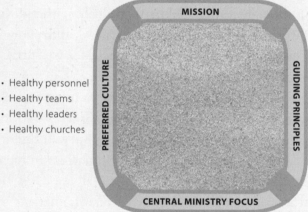

We exist to glorify God by multiplying healthy churches among all people

MISSION

PREFERRED CULTURE

GUIDING PRINCIPLES

CENTRAL MINISTRY FOCUS

- Healthy personnel
- Healthy teams
- Healthy leaders
- Healthy churches

- Word based and Spirit empowered
- Team led and team driven
- Partnership driven
- Empowered personnel
- Entrepreneurial thinking
- Measure effectiveness
- Multiplication not addition
- Learning organization
- Resourced well
- Holistic and integrated in approach

To develop, empower, and release healthy ReachGlobal personnel and healthy national leaders

Life International Sandbox

To multiply healthy, Christ-centered, life-giving
ministries wherever abortion exists around the world

- Practicing intimacy before impact
- Practicing the sanctity of human life
- Practicing a biblical sexuality
- Practicing a kingdom life-giving lifestyle
- Practicing forgiveness, grace, and mercy

MISSION

PREFERRED CULTURE

GUIDING PRINCIPLES

CENTRAL MINISTRY FOCUS

- We are Spirit empowered and Word based
- We are prayer led
- We are evangelistically compelled
- We are team led and team driven
- We are partnership driven
- We measure effectiveness
- We practice multiplication not addition
- We resource for maximum ministry
- We take a holistic approach

To equip, empower, and release healthy
leaders for life-giving ministries

DESIGNING YOUR SANDBOX

The sandbox helps you visualize and communicate in a simple format the most important aspects of your organization. It defines the ministry philosophy and the culture you are intentionally creating.

The sandbox simplifies the complexities of your organization and provides clarity about who you are—all with one simple picture. Ambiguous and complicated systems hurt otherwise good organizations! If you cannot quickly, clearly, and simply explain who you are, your own people will often not get it—to say nothing of those outside your ministry. The sandbox allows everyone to see and remember what you are all about.

H. I. QUESTIONS FOR TEAM DISCUSSION

Which of the four sides of the sandbox have you already clarified for your ministry?

Are there sides you think you should clarify for the sake of your ministry?

Do you think building a sandbox would help leaders, staff, and constituents better understand what you are about? Discuss your perceptions with your team.

Take a few minutes on your own to try to identify what a sandbox for your organization would look like. Then share your results with the team.

CHAPTER FIVE

HEALTHY TEAM LEADERS

CHAPTER SUMMARY:

Teams will only be as good as the leaders who lead them.

Good leaders have made the transition from being an independent producer to leading through a team. They have an attitude that "it is no longer about me but about us." They have made the shift from "How I would do things" to empowering good people to do things as they would — in line with their gifting and skills. They have transitioned from "hands-on" in the details to helping define the large issues and allowing others to take care of the details.

Healthy leaders intentionally take a servant role and prioritize the health and results of the team, not their own status or power. This allows them to hire or recruit people who are even better than they are.

Healthy leaders pay attention to the five priorities of every leader:

1. *Personal development* — Ensuring they live intentionally in their spiritual, emotional, relational, and professional life
2. *Strategic leadership* — Providing strategic leadership to the organization or the part of the organization they lead
3. *Strong team* — Building a healthy, unified, aligned, strategic, and results-oriented team
4. *Leadership development* — Developing current and future leaders

5. *Mobilizing resources* — Mobilizing resources necessary for the team's ministry to flourish.

And, they manage their dark sides.

Many pastors and ministry leaders did not sign up to lead others. They heard the call of God, wanted to make a difference for His kingdom, and entered ministry. For some, it was a shock to wake up one day and realize, "I've got to lead a staff!" As one pastor of a church of eight hundred put it to me, "T. J., I now have ten staff members and I really don't like leading them. I love to preach but I don't like the job of leading staff—and some of them are a real pain. Help!"

This pastor loved to do what he signed up to do: preach. Because he was good at it, he found himself in a growing church with multiple staff members. Now he sensed the stakes were higher and he needed to lead better, but he did not know how. Countless Christian leaders and pastors feel the same way and face the same challenge.

Since good team leadership is usually learned, my word to leaders who are reading this chapter is this: Don't be intimidated and don't judge yourself as you read. Look for areas where you can grow as a team leader. There are no perfect leaders, only good leaders who constantly grow their leadership ability.

GOOD LEADERS TRANSITION FROM INDEPENDENT PRODUCER TO LEADING THROUGH A TEAM

The transition from independent producer to leading a staff is not without its bumps and its lessons because the two responsibilities are very different. I remember when I was an independent producer. I was a staff of one with an assistant. My schedule was my own, and I could focus where I wanted to focus. While my work affected others, I was not personally responsible for them. Today, the picture is different. I have a staff of more than five hundred with ten senior leaders who directly or indirectly report to me. My priorities and how I spend my time directly affects others—and my ability to lead them well.

Life for an independent producer is fairly simple. Life for a leader of a staff or team is much more complex. Moving from one to the other requires making critical transitions in how leaders think and act. They must transition:

- From thinking about "How I drive ministry myself" to "How I drive ministry through others." It is no longer about "me" as much as "us."
- From "How I would do things" to "Empowering other people to do things as they would."
- From "I can do life as I like to arrange it" to "I need to take into account all those on my team and how I can serve them and help them become the best they can be."
- From "I'm the one out on the court playing" to "I coach the people who make the plays." It is not possible to ignore my team. If I do, their attitude deteriorates or we develop silos without alignment.
- From "I am hands-on in the details" to "I help define the big issues and allow others to take care of the details."
- From "*I* can determine the plan and strategy" to "*We* need to determine and own a common strategy."
- From "I have a meeting to attend" to "I have a meeting I need to carefully prepare for and lead."
- From "My opinion is the one that counts" to "I need to be collaborative in my thinking and decision making" and "I need to encourage robust dialogue and take a nondefensive posture when others disagree with mc."

These transitions are not easy, but they are necessary. There is significant organizational pain—and even attrition—when leaders are required to move from being solo producers to team leaders and don't understand they now need to work differently. It is not uncommon for pastors who have not made these transitions to face considerable unhappiness or conflict with staff. Often they are not aware of why the conflict is occurring.

A true story. Jon is a gifted communicator and evangelist and has excellent relational skills. Based on those gifts, he was the first pastor of a wonderful church in a professional, upscale community that has a good number of executive and CEO-type retirees. The makeup of his church board reflects this executive mentality.

Jon is gregarious, impulsive, likes to do things himself, and resists any kind of schedule. His gifting allowed him to get a lot done without much planning. Because he is an effective communicator, those who come to the church love what he does from the pulpit along with his outgoing, highly relational style.

All of this worked well for Jon until the church hit about six hundred or so. Then tension grew between Jon and his board and staff. From the board's perspective, it was time to bring greater cohesion, planning, and organization to what had been run like a mom-and-pop shop. Besides, they had just moved into a new facility from a rented one, and that inherently required better organization. They loved Jon dearly, which was in his favor, but felt something had to change. To put it bluntly, Jon's leaders were or had been highly disciplined executives and Jon was a "fly by the seat of his pants" kind of guy, which became irritating to his board members.

Jon's relationships with his staff developed fissures as well. Staff members often did not know where Jon was or what he was doing (he did not tell them and did not keep a written schedule). They did not feel they were being coached in their jobs (they didn't even have job descriptions to define what was expected of them). Because Jon spent little quality time with staff, they felt alone and devalued. It did not go without notice that Jon spent more quality time with congregants than his own staff—whom he was supposed to be leading.

Because Jon was a creative guy, he would often come up with a new idea at the last minute and expect staff to respond. Meetings were about Jon talking to staff rather than team dialogue. He was such a great communicator (debater) that they felt they would lose the argument when they disagreed with him (and they had plenty of experience).

All of this came to a point where I was called in as a consultant. After interviewing the board, staff, and Jon, I shared with him some of their frustrations and how he was perceived. Jon immediately protested, "But this is who I am."

I responded that if he wanted to continue to grow the church, he needed to make critical transitions in his thought and practice — to go from an independent producer to a team leader. Otherwise he would become a barrier to the church moving forward, and the conflict would grow. The other alternative would be for him to start another church where he could be an independent producer, grow it to five hundred or so, and then pass it off to someone who enjoyed leading a team.

Jon decided he wanted to make the transition, difficult as it was, and the leadership quietly hired an executive coach to help him. Several years later he is still there, and life is calmer and more peaceful.

Jon's pain is not unique; some don't survive the transition. When we ask people to take on the leadership of others it is critical that we help them understand the transition they must move through. It is a transition of values, roles, how one does life, how one views and builds a team, what one's priorities and schedule are, and how well one defines the organization and where it is going. Then we must help them make those transitions. Too often, we leave people to their own devices, assuming they will figure it out — a strategy guaranteed to cause pain to both the leader and the team. Moses was a leader who had to make such a transition and needed the help of a coach (the story is in Exodus 18).

We have recognized in ReachGlobal that careful coaching is required when we ask someone who has primarily been doing hands-on ministry to become a leader. The tendency is to continue the hands-on ministry and add on the leadership piece. Yet, with each successive step into leadership comes a cost: We must leave something behind if we are going to be successful in the new role.

Flying at the right altitude. A way to think about this is to determine the altitude leaders must fly at in their leadership role. As the leader of ReachGlobal, my responsibility is to fly at 40,000 feet so I can see the horizons from the best vantage point. My senior team members need to be at 30,000 feet and their area leaders at 20,000 feet; many others will be at ground level.

When I default to flying lower than I should by getting into issues someone else should be dealing with, I am compromising my leadership and have likely defaulted to old habits and old responsibilities. My job is not to deal with 20,000-foot issues but with 40,000-foot issues.

Joel is a leader who rose through the ranks of a ministry organization to become a senior leader. He started as a missionary "on the ground," then became a team leader, soon an area leader, and then a senior leader. He needed to be flying at 30,000 feet, but there were things he loved to do at the 5,000-foot level. He had a habit of "losing altitude" to get into things he used to do. Yet he was now responsible for a huge area of the world, scores of missionaries, and many national partnerships.

His leader had to coach him to stay at 30,000 feet. Could he still do the things he used to do? Not personally. If he wanted those projects done he had to find someone to do them *through* rather than doing them himself. With coaching and practice he learned to stay at the right altitude.

This does not mean leaders are aloof or distant from those they lead. We are always with those we lead. It does mean we are doing tasks appropriate for our current roles and have given up things appropriate for past roles. We cannot take on new responsibility—and do it well—without giving up old responsibility. Further, when we hang on to the old tasks, we disempower those who should be responsible for them. Remember, healthy leaders make the transition from independent producer to leading through others. The transition-related pain of loss is a natural result of agreeing to fly at a higher altitude. (We will discuss this more fully in chapter 9.)

When pastors like Jon or leaders like Joel micromanage staff and continue to do what they used to do, they are flying at the wrong altitude. Healthy leaders understand the altitude they need to fly at and stay there.

H. I. MOMENT

Reflect on your transition from independent producer to a leader of others. What were the tough spots?

H. I. BEST PRACTICE

People making this kind of transition should find others who have successfully navigated the change and ask them for coaching. Ask what "dumb tax" they paid (things they would do differently in the future) and what personal and professional changes they needed to make. Having a coach can save pain and make the transition smoother.

HEALTHY LEADERS VALUE INFLUENCE AND RESULTS OVER STATUS AND POWER

One of the tests of great leadership is whether a leader needs the spotlight, adulation, or credit for the results of the team's work. Power, status, and praise are a deadly aphrodisiac for unhealthy leaders. These leaders are often charismatic and visionary but are seldom able to build a strong team because, ultimately, the work and ministry is always about them. Insecure or narcissist leaders require that they be the center, essentially stealing credit from those who were actually responsible. And don't be fooled. People notice, especially the team who made it happen! Unfortunately too many of these leaders find their way into ministry. Stay away from them. Eventually they implode, causing pain for those around them — and it is ugly when it comes apart.

To be a good team leader one must intentionally take on a servant role and prioritize the health and results of the team. While every organization has lines of authority, healthy teams work with an egalitarian ethos, where all sit at the table as peers with the ability to make an equal contribution. Leaders, like Jon, who dominate meetings don't get it and send the message that the team is about "me" not "us."

Commitment to working as a team means we give away credit for accomplishments. We intentionally lift up team members, allowing our influence to flow through them so they have the authority to do what they must in the organization.

The job of the team leader is to empower others, to be their coach and cheerleader, and to allow them to see the fruits of their work. A team, when working together, can see results that are a quantum leap from what the leader could produce alone. Status and power are not important to good leaders; influence and results are. Good leaders give others the praise for successes and take personal responsibility for failures.

HEALTHY LEADERS BUILD TEAMS MORE COMPETENT THAN THEMSELVES

Think about that for a moment! To be willing to build a team of people who can do their tasks better than you could do them takes a lot of personal security, a commitment to mission, and a deep resolve to build the best team for the best ministry results. Insecure leaders hire less competent people because those who are strong threaten them. They want the final word, and strong people (appropriately) will challenge the status quo.

This is one of the shifts in thinking we need to make when we move from independent producer to leading through a team. We will only be as good as our team. Therefore, our ministry success reflects the quality of the team. Our role is like an orchestra director who ensures great musicians are recruited and are playing from the same musical score at the same tempo.

My own leader is a master at this, and I have deep respect for him. He has assembled a great team, is not intimidated by us, and allows us to play to our strengths. If you have served on a team with that kind of leader you know how wonderful it is.

As you build your team, look for the very best people you can find. Generally if they are not more qualified than you would be in their roles, you have the wrong people. Give these people freedom in their responsibilities; you cannot give great guidance in an area that is not your strength. You can outline outcomes, but you must empower them to figure out strategy—which is why you need people who are great at what they do. I am not a great detail person so I hired the very best: Lindsay, who "runs my life." I can give her feedback on what success looks like for her, but if I had to tell her how to do what she needs to do, I would have hired the wrong person.

It should be obvious by now that the Emotional Intelligence (EQ) of the team leader plays a major role in developing and maintaining healthy teams. The better we know ourselves and the healthier our EQs, the better leaders we will be.

HEALTHY LEADERS FOCUS ON FIVE KEY RESPONSIBILITIES

Good leaders must do at least five things well. These responsibilities are the highest priorities in one's leadership role. How well they are done will determine the effectiveness of the team.

Pastors who read this may push back and say, "I do a lot of other things." That is true. But in your *leadership* role, the following five responsibilities are critical. (In chapter 7, we will talk about the necessity of committing to develop and follow an annual plan for each of these priorities.)

1. Personal development—Ensuring you live intentionally in your spiritual, family, emotional, relational, and professional lives. By personal development, I mean the core issues that make and keep a leader. These become the leaders' highest priorities because health in these areas determines their ability to lead spiritually and professionally and to model the kind of faithful, fruitful, connected life the New Testament describes. There are six areas of personal development to take into account:

1. Marriage (if married)
2. Children (if you have them)
3. Relationship with Christ (keeping it vital)
4. Understanding yourself and your wiring (EQ)

5. Professional development
6. Your skill as a leader

These areas of development go to a core truth: Healthy leaders pay close attention to their own lives so they can lead out of spiritual, emotional, and relational health. As the apostle Paul wrote to Timothy, "Watch your life and doctrine closely" (1 Timothy 4:16). The higher the level of leadership one has, the greater the temptation to take short cuts in personal development because the leadership demands become so heavy. Those who take shortcuts pay heavy consequences when marriages come apart, hidden addictions become known, relationships suffer from neglect, professional growth stops, or spiritual temperature wanes.

Just as Christian leaders seek to understand God and His Word, they also need to understand themselves—areas of strength and areas of weakness. The better we understand how we are wired, where we have blind spots, and where and when we are vulnerable to sin, the healthier we will be.

All of us have a "dark side." The dark side includes areas where we are vulnerable to temptation, unresolved emotional issues that spill out and hurt others, uncontrolled anger, selfishness leading to narcissism, poor treatment of those we lead, or other issues that affect our lives and cause spiritual, emotional, or relational ruptures. Dark sides must be dealt with. Otherwise they will cause us and others pain and threaten our ability to lead.

I have a good friend who pastors a church of four hundred on the Gulf Coast. He is a good pastor. But he is also driven, never content with where the church is, and not inwardly happy. He worries constantly that the church is not growing the way it ought to be. Because he is insecure about his success (as measured by church growth), he tends to be insecure when staff or board members differ with him on strategy or ministry priorities. The insecurity can manifest as defensiveness.

My friend's dark side shows up in his discontent, unhappiness, unquenchable drive, and lack of self-confidence. And it has an impact on his staff. If he is never content, he will never be content with what his staff does. If he is not a happy person, the lack of happiness will spill over on to them. If he feels success is measured primarily by fast church growth, so will his staff.

These internal issues cause my friend anxiety, cause conflict with the board, and affect those he leads. In addition, his family pays the price, as he is often mulling on his anxiety and not fully present for them.

Fortunately he is on a quest to figure out these issues, which most likely can be traced back to his family of origin, but which are spiritual as well. Unresolved, they will haunt him and affect his family and those he works with. The fact that he is now aware of the issues means he can work on mitigating their effects.

Understanding our wirings, motivations, dark sides, and personal dysfunctions sets us on a path of personal growth that is crucial to leading well. The path is not always pleasant, but it is necessary.

Leaders who make the six areas of personal growth central to their lives will develop the emotional, spiritual, relational, and professional health needed to lead well.

H. I. MOMENT

Make some notes to yourself about your dark side: What lives in your dark side? What are you doing about it? How does it affect your family and those you lead? Are there areas you need to pay attention to? What are you going to do about it?

Do not neglect your dark side!

2. Strategic leadership — Providing strategic leadership to the organization or the part of the organization you lead. How do leaders provide strategic leadership? First, they are the keepers of the vision. They always pull the team back to the mission. Without a leader who constantly reminds the team of its primary purpose, mission drift takes place and activity starts to replace results.

In chapter 1, we made the case that high-impact teams are deeply missional. Good leaders are always seeking results that are consistent with the mission. This is not about administrating the team. Leaders do some administration, but they are not administrators. Rather, they are always pushing the mission forward—an emphasis that often gets lost in the press of activity.

Second, leaders ask lots of questions: How can we do this better? Why do we do what we do in the way we do it? What are others doing that we should know about? Are we all pulling in the same direction? Good leaders know that conventional wisdom and methods are often not productive and they continually question their effectiveness. They are always asking questions, probing, and looking for new ways of thinking about the problems they face. One of my indicators of how good a leader someone is relates to how many questions he or she asks. Both one-on-one and in a team setting, leaders use questions to clarify issues, learn from others, and come to workable solutions and new strategies. If asking questions is not a natural trait for you, work on it and you will be amazed at the results.

Third, leaders must regularly break from activity and do nothing but think! Strategic leadership means taking the time to ponder, muse, and pray about the ministry, the mission, and how the team can more effectively deliver on the mission. The tyranny of the urgent keeps many leaders and teams from being as effective as they could be. Busyness kills thinking time.

Fourth, through written agendas for meetings, leaders keep the important issues in front of the team. Because leaders set the agenda for their teams, they determine how often teams focuses on strategic issues related to the mission. This is why carefully planned and well-executed meetings are critical. What we do in meetings determines how missional the team is.

Finally, leaders help their teams determine what they should do next to drive the mission forward. This involves key strategic initiatives that will provide significant leverage.[1] At any one time, every organization should be engaged in three to five strategic initiatives that are moving the mission forward.

Strategic leadership is about keeping the mission of the organization central and the team aligned toward accomplishing the mission. This is a core responsibility of anyone who leads a team. Those of us who have served on ineffective teams know they were often the result of leaders who did not take strategic leadership seriously.

3. Strong team—Building a healthy, unified, aligned, strategic, and results-oriented team. Never underestimate the importance of strong team or your responsibility to build a healthy, unified, aligned, strategic, and results-oriented team. Your ability to advance the mission is directly dependent on the people who make up your team. We ignore strong team at our peril.

Why do I stress this so strongly? Because many leaders do not take teams seriously! I have consulted with numerous churches, many of them large (attendance of more than one thousand). The senior pastors are good communicators and often have great vision. Too often, however, they have ignored building a strong team. Even if they have good people, the staff and leaders are often not unified around a common vision in alignment with one another and the senior pastor.

Strong team requires attention to four areas. The first is *getting the right people in the right seats*. We will discuss this in the next chapter.

The second area is *maximum missional clarity*. When we are foggy on our mission, alignment or missional unity is not possible—team members are not sure what it is! Good leaders constantly clarify why we are here and where we are going. Vince Lombardi, the famous football coach, would start each season with a simple lesson. He would hold up a football and say, "This is a football." He constantly communicated the basics. In chapter 2, we saw how leaders can keep their teams aligned if they clarify what the organization is all about.

What is your "football"? Why does your team exist? Are all team members clear on what the end result is? If you live and talk the mission—all the time—your team will get it.

The third area that is key to strong team is the leader's *willingness to empower* team members to "do their thing." Micromanagement and control kill strong teams. I have a great friend who leads a very effective ministry he founded. He is a classic entrepreneur who feels a need to have his hand in everything. He is in need of key staff members, but when he hires at a senior level, the new staffers often do not last long. It is not that he doesn't find good people. The problem is that he *does*—and then these good people find they have no freedom to do what they were hired to do. Everything must be vetted by the founder. Even though they love their leader and the mission of the organization, they find no joy in working in a disempowered environment.

When pastors like Jon, whom I mentioned earlier in the chapter, come up with great new ideas that staff members must respond to (at the last minute), they disempower their staff, who have been working diligently on their areas of responsibility. This does not mean leaders cannot speak into "what" or "how" a team member is doing. The issue is how the leader does it; the input should empower those on the team rather than disempower them.

Controlling leaders (and there are many) may attract good people if their vision is significant (good people love great vision), but they will not keep those people. If you feel you must control your team, you either have the wrong people on the team or you have a hard time empowering others. Leaders who empower develop extremely loyal team members.

One of the issues related to empowerment is removing barriers that prevent team members from carrying out their responsibilities. A barrier may be political, it may be a person who is not playing ball, or it may be the lack of resources. Every month I ask my team members two questions designed to get to this issue: "What do you need from me?" and "What barriers are you facing that you need to have removed?"

Building strong team takes time, and it will not happen unless it becomes a priority of the team leader. When it comes together, however, working with the team is a dream and a joy.

The fourth area essential to a strong team is for the leader to take *the posture of a mentor*. As a team leader, you are most likely the supervisor of those on the team. Yet people primarily need someone to coach and mentor them. Team members need to know their leader believes in them, wants the best for them, and will develop, empower, and release them. Leaders who do this develop long-term, loyal, and healthy team members.

What is the cost? Time! Mentoring and coaching mean at least a monthly meeting combined with ongoing availability. In a later chapter, we will discuss how to do this in an empowering way. While it takes time to be a mentor/coach, the ministry results will be huge. Remember that your success is directly dependent on the success of those on your team. The more you pour into them, the more successful they will be.

H. I. MOMENT

Do you gravitate toward empowerment or control/micromanagement with your staff members? How do you think your team members would answer?

Can you think of any areas where you disempower your team? Are you willing to ask your team to respond to your level of empowerment?

4. Leadership development—Developing current and future leaders. Pastors, church leaders, and organizational leaders: Are you developing current and future leaders for your ministry? It amazes me how many churches and organizations have no plan to develop leaders—and then wonder why they have trouble when new leaders create problems. Leaders pay close attention to identifying and developing leaders for the future. As the leader of an organization spread across the globe, I am convinced ReachGlobal will only be as good as its leaders. Why? Because good leaders attract the best people, who flourish under empowering leadership.

While I am blessed with a dream team in the two top leadership levels of the organization (and a great staff of missionaries), I am constantly asking three questions: "Who will replace these leaders if they were to leave?" "Where is my bench and who is on it?" and "What are we doing to find and develop potential leaders?" I will have failed if I do not raise up the next generation of leaders so the organization flourishes in the future.

Whether you serve in a church or other ministry, there are significant advantages in raising new leaders from within your organization when you can. Insiders know who you are, they understand your vision and mission, and they know the culture. Because they are insiders, you can mentor them before they get into a leadership position.

In ReachGlobal, we have developed curriculum to develop new leaders for all key positions. I give personal attention to developing leaders for the two senior teams of the organization. In addition, we never meet as a senior team without a significant learning component included. I suggest you articulate a strategy for identifying and developing new team members and make a periodic place in your calendar to review your progress against the strategy. Remember, we will only be as good as the team who works with us.

Every team, church, or organization is only one leadership generation away from decline unless the next generation of leaders is intentionally being developed. Each generation of leaders holds in their hands the responsibility to nurture the next generation.

H. I. BEST PRACTICE

Ask every team member to identify and develop someone who could take his or her place. Hold team members accountable for this on an annual basis. In the best case scenario you develop qualified people for all key positions. In the event a team member moves on, you have replacement options available from inside the organization.

5. Mobilizing resources—Mobilizing key resources necessary for the ministry of your team to flourish. Team leaders mobilize people, strategies, finances, and other needed resources. Leaders use their authority and position to ensure team members have the resources needed to fulfill their responsibilities. Leaders are always asking their team, "What do you need to get your job done?" Then they help find the resources or point people in the right direction.

This may mean negotiating for cooperation from other departments or for budgets. Sometimes it means finding donors to help fund specific ministry projects. Mobilizing resources is not simply about funding, however. Resources can involve strategic partnerships with those who have expertise or ministry resources. Resources might include events where you bring together people to exchange ideas and best practices. Resources might be practitioners who can help your team think through opportunities.

One great, untapped resource for ministry teams is workplace professionals. Engaging them to help us think strategically and find solutions to problems is huge leverage. Because of their different perspective, they will often think of solutions we would never dream of. Leaders are always on the lookout for strategies that might work or people who can contribute to the mission. All too often we try to reinvent wheels. Why pay a "dumb tax" that others have already paid? Why not learn from those who have figured out what you are trying to figure out?

The central point is that we want to be networked with others, know what is working, and understand "pretty good practices." Leaders help their team grapple with needed resources and point them in productive directions.

A WORD TO PASTORS

Everything we do as leaders of teams revolves around these five key areas of responsibility. Paying attention to them will help us lead well and will serve our teams well.

If you are a pastor and are not yet practicing these five leadership responsibilities with your team, it is important to talk with your board to ensure they will support the time and effort needed to do this well. Your ability to lead well depends on your investment in your team, so it is crucial for your board to support that investment. You may want to have them read select chapters in this book.

H. I. QUESTIONS FOR TEAM LEADERS

Are you comfortable with the fact that your team will only be as good as the leadership you provide?

Where are you in the process of moving from individual producer to leading through a team?

In which of the five key responsibilities of a leader do you excel?

Which of the five key responsibilities of a leader need more of your attention?

Are you willing to dialogue with your team on these issues so that you can be a better leader for them?

Are you flying at the correct altitude for your leadership role?

LEADER'S SCORECARD

Give yourself a grade (A, B, or C) in the following areas:

_____I have made the transition from independent producer to leading through a team.

_____I am flying at the right altitude.

_____I am intentional in my spiritual life.

_____I am intentional in my family life.

_____I have intentional growth in my professional life.

_____I manage my "dark side."

_____I regularly keep the mission in front of my team.

_____I constantly ask questions.

_____I regularly take time away to think.

_____My team members are in the right seats.

_____I provide maximum missional clarity to the team.

_____I empower staff rather than control or micromanage them.

_____I intentionally mentor/coach my team members (at least monthly).

_____I have an intentional plan to develop new leaders.

_____Mobilization of resources is high on my list.

_____My schedule is designed to allow me to lead with excellence.

CHAPTER SIX

BUILDING A HEALTHY TEAM

CHAPTER SUMMARY:

High-impact teams are built deliberately — over time.

Not all people are right for your team.

Potential or current team members can be categorized as A-team, B-team, or C-team players. This is not about being a good or bad person but about the ability to play well on your team. C-team players do not belong on your team no matter how nice they are or how long they have been with the organization. They have a fatal flaw that will compromise the work of the team.

In choosing team members, leaders never negotiate the crucial issues of character and good EQ. They take their time and pay the price to determine a good fit before they hire because they understand the principle of "Pay now or pay more later." They do not make hiring decisions alone.

In the hiring or recruiting process, leaders make a "need to know" list of things they must know about potential team members and things potential members need to know about leaders, teams, and team expectations.

Healthy ministries are never static; therefore, good leaders continue to grow the capacity of teams through ongoing training. They are exegetes of the people they lead so that members are deployed in their "sweet spots."

Leaders build their teams, one member at a time, and build the capacity of the team through ongoing training. They never neglect the team!

High-impact teams are built deliberately—over time. The process is not easy and takes time and attention. But the payoff is *huge*! Finding people who fit your team and getting them into the right places is one of your most important tasks as a leader. Nobody will get it right all the time, but if you can get it right *most* of the time your happiness factor will be high.

GETTING THE RIGHT PEOPLE

While getting the right people into the right places may seem obvious, many leaders do not spend enough time reflecting on who would be the right people for their ministries. There are many good and competent people who will not fit *your* team. Others will look great but have fatal flaws that will cause headaches. Getting the right people in the right seats affects two outcomes: growing the capacity of your ministry and avoiding unnecessary pain for you and the organization. If you lead a team, you have probably felt the pain!

A-team, B-team, and C-team players. Potential or current team members can be categorized as playing on teams of different levels. These categories are not about labeling them as good or bad people but describing their ability to play well on your team.

A-team players are self-directed, hard working, self-starters, highly competent, and committed to team. They are dedicated to your values and mission and are results oriented. A-team players have high EQs, work well with others, and have good self-awareness.

B-team players work hard, buy in to your values and mission, are committed to teamwork, are results oriented, and have high EQ, but they may require more direction. Generally, B-team players are not as creative or entrepreneurial as A-team players but will do their jobs diligently and faithfully, given concrete direction.

C-team players may or may not be competent (some are very competent and may even be "stars"). But they have a fatal flaw that disqualifies them. Disqualifiers include lack of tangible results, laziness, lack of buy in or adherence to your mission or values, low EQ that disrupts relationships, inability to work productively as a team player, or immaturity that requires constant management.

A- and B-team folks are the heart of any good team and organization. Know which players you need and work to fill positions based on that need. In some higher-level jobs, you will need A-team players. In many jobs, a solid, faithful B player is exactly what you need.

Let me say boldly what many Christians are unwilling to say: C players do not belong on our teams no matter how nice they are or how long they have been with the organization. Allowing them to stay condemns the rest of the team to frustration and compromises your mission. Remember, we are using God's resources to further God's kingdom. We have a responsibility to the kingdom, to our donors, and to the organization to deliver on mission.

Before you decide people are C players, consider whether they have ever been coached or mentored and whether anyone has ever been honest with them regarding the problems. If not, you owe it to them to put them through a process to see if they can be helped to move up to a B level.

It is possible that people producing C-level results are in the wrong job or "seat." Then you may want to do some testing and try an alternate job if one is available. What is not wise is to leave an incompetent person in place. Your credibility as a leader will be legitimately tarnished if you do not deal with performance issues — or other fatal flaws.

Another reality of organizational life is that someone who is an A or B player at one phase of an organization's development can slip to a B or C at another. Most people have built-in "capacity ceilings" where they cease to be effective. Perhaps they are not able to multiply so they can lead a larger number of people, or they may just have quit growing (an all too common scenario). Thus a youth worker who was a star when she had twenty youth in her group starts to slip when she has sixty. She could personally relate to twenty; she cannot relate to sixty and is not able to build a team to help her.

If coaching and mentoring do not solve the issues with C players, you may have to move these team members to other seats on your bus or help them, redemptively, find seats on another bus. What you cannot do is allow them to function at a substandard level without directly affecting the rest of your team and your ministry results.

H. I. BEST PRACTICE

Follow HR protocol in addressing performance issues, but once you know the situation is not going to change, act as quickly as you can to move the person off your team and perhaps out of your organization so you minimize pain. Do so in a way that is gracious, defensible, and as redemptive as possible, but do not ignore the issue.

One organization I consulted with employed a brilliant individual who created such continual relational problems that no one in the organization wanted to work with her. Yet her job was in a service division that required her to work across departments. There was no doubt about her capacity, competency, or agreement with the mission, but her low EQ created major trust issues even for her boss (why didn't he do something?) and for the division he ran (they were delivering bad service). Even after the organization provided executive coaching at significant expense, her behavior patterns did not change; the organization finally had to let her go. They probably should not have waited as long as they did, as the relational chaos and subsequent lack of trust took several years to overcome.

You may think what I have written here is harsh and lacks grace. But think about this: Your first responsibility as a leader is to ensure the health of your organization while always acting redemptively when a change is needed. People who are not doing well are usually not in their sweet spots, and they often know it. To leave them there is not fair to the organization and others on your team, nor is it in the best interest of the people who cannot play at the required level.

Never compromise on critical issues. Especially when hiring, it is tempting to overlook character issues. Sometimes the person's competency and what he or she can bring to the team overshadows potential problems. That is a fatal mistake for a leader in any organization, but especially in a Christian ministry where character goes to the heart of credibility. If there is any question on the character issue, walk away!

Others have great Christian character but don't have the right competencies or EQ. I am always amazed when someone without the competencies or EQ is recommended with the statement, "Well, he is a really nice Christian and wants to work for a Christian organization." (For some, working for a nice Christian organization means they could not make it in the secular world or are looking for personal needs to be met.)

Be clear on the Key Result Areas (KRAs) and competencies. When you are hiring, job descriptions are not enough. They simply describe the activities the position entails. What you need to focus on are the *end results* the position requires. For all positions there ought to be three to five clearly defined results that, if fulfilled, will spell success (see chapter 7 for more information on KRAs).

Once you know what spells success, you can determine the core competencies an individual must possess. Many things are negotiable in hiring and will be determined by the wiring and gifting of the individual. What is not negotiable are the core competencies, since without these there is no chance for the prospective hire to succeed.

Understand the principle "Pay now or pay more later." The longer I lead and the more people I hire, the more convinced I am of the wisdom of thorough testing before hiring (I've paid plenty of dumb tax for not doing it enough). We often don't do testing and due diligence because it costs money or we are in such a hurry or we choose to be optimistic and hope for the best.

Here is the reality. You either pay now and spend the time and money to ensure the competence of your potential hire, or you pay dearly later through the pain of letting someone go — often after enduring months or years of performance issues. Untold frustration would be avoided if we would take the long-term view and ensure the best fit by spending what we need before we hire.

If the candidate will be playing at a senior level in the organization or church, it pays to put individuals through the same executive testing any good secular organization would use. (At the end of this chapter you will find recommendations for tests that can be helpful in learning about your candidate's wiring.) This will help measure capacity, leadership skills, conflict resolution skills, and EQ.

A key reason for the best testing you can do is that you want to understand people's sweet spots before you hire them. Their sweet spots include how they like to be managed, how they manage others, how they like to work (individually or on a team), their driving values and passions, and where they have been successful in the past (past behavior is the best indicator of future behavior). The more you know about individuals' wiring, the better you will be able to coach and position them on your team.

H. I. BEST PRACTICE

Never make a hiring decision by yourself. Ask those who know you best and who have good discernment to interview people you are thinking of hiring. Do multiple interviews and listen to the gut reaction of those you bring into the process. Include both male and female interviewers to see how both react. Be wary of hiring if people you trust express cautions. They are probably seeing something you don't see (or don't want to see).

If you are hiring for a senior position, consider going to candidates' homes and spending a day with them. You will be amazed at what you learn about them, their marriages (if married), and their family relationships. Remember, pay now or pay more later!

Make the "need to know" list. Make two lists when you are adding someone to your team: what you need to know about the candidate and what the candidate needs to know about you, your team, and your ministry. Neither of you wants surprises after hiring!

You need to know wiring, background, competency, character, culture fit, work style, level the candidate can play at, passions, values, and whatever else is important to you.

Candidates need to understand your leadership style; how you do team; expectations you and the organization hold for the position; the organization's values, mission, and preferred future; the culture of your ministry; what candidates can or cannot expect from you as the leader; and other significant issues that define the organization. Be brutally transparent so they know the upside and downside of your organization. If your honesty scares them away, they are the wrong hire.

H. I. BEST PRACTICE

When you hire, have the candidate meet with and interview several people you currently lead and who know you well so the candidate can understand how you are wired, how you lead, and what they can expect from you. Often those around us can give a better explanation of who we are and how we lead than we can.

Always check references. It is wise to get references at least two layers deep. You can expect the first list of references, which the candidate gives you, to be positive. Never completely trust the feedback unless you personally know those people. Ask each reference for the names of one or two additional people who would know the candidate well and then contact that layer. This lets you explore whether what you know about the candidate is true and if he or she would fit your organization.

When discussing the fit of the candidate, be sure to describe the culture of your organization, your management and leadership style, and your expectations for the position. Someone may be competent but not fit your culture. Those who know the candidate best will be able to give feedback on the cultural and expectations fit.

You want to explore additional issues before you hire or reposition people from within the organization, such as:

- Do they have high EQ?
- Are they team players?
- Can they play at the level of the other members on the team?
- Do they have skills that will complement the team?

- Will they contribute to the whole rather than simply guard individual turf?
- Do they fully embrace the mission and values of the organization?
- Do the other members of the team think they will fit well?
- Do they have the expertise needed for the ministries in which they will participate?
- Do they understand the implications of joining the team and the expectations for them as team members?
- What level of leadership and management support will they need from you?
- If they will lead others, do their leadership styles fit your organization's leadership culture?

When hiring from the marketplace for a ministry role. I am a great fan of bringing people from the marketplace into ministry organizations and have done it a number of times. However, sharp differences in culture between the marketplace and Christian organizations (and nonprofits in general) can complicate the marriage.

At the risk of oversimplification, the marketplace is often a bottom-line place (it's about financial results) with less than collegial relationships, has far more discipline for results (it's about the bottom line), and can be a rather unforgiving environment (which is why so many senior executives retire early). Ministry organizations tend to be less driven by the bottom line (and less disciplined for results), are more collegial and gracious, and have a very different culture (for good or bad).

The transition from marketplace to ministry can be a shock to the system for everyone. One search firm I work with has watched this system shock many times and concluded that coaching in the transition is critical. One of my problematic hires had worked for a major Fortune 500 corporation. He did very well in the interviews, but once on board he managed to alienate almost everyone at his level or below with his crass, condescending attitude. He never could cope with the collegial and gracious culture of our organization. Several times he described to me the knockdown verbal fights he observed among senior vice presidents at his previous employer (his idea of robust dialogue, I guess). When I suggested he be more collegial, he responded that we just were not "honest." I said we were "honest but gracious." After executive coaching did not change anything, he moved on at our invitation.

A new hire does not have to have an EQ issue like this to struggle with the transition from marketplace to ministry. It pays to be aware of the issues in such a transition and monitor closely so that it goes well.

After the hire. Your positions are filled, and you breathe a sigh of relief. But not so fast! Now the real work begins. From day one, you want to ensure new team members understand the mission, values, preferred future, and all the things you communicated from your "what the candidate needs to know" list. New hires have heard you; now you need to make sure they "get it" in terms of how it will affect their work on your team. The more personal time you can spend on the front end, the faster the new team members will get up to speed rather than trying to figure out the "rules" by watching others. Make personal introductions to those they need to know.

Set aside regular times over the first six months just to sit down together and talk. Ask what they are observing, what they are surprised about, what information they need to do their jobs, and how you can remove barriers. Ask them how they read the culture of your team and ministry. They are new—you might be surprised by what they observe with new sets of eyes. Probe with questions so you both learn and understand how they are assimilating into the organization.

For your own purposes and so you can do a better job next time, after six months ask new hires to tell you what they wish they had been told on the front end, what the most difficult part of their transitions was, and what was most helpful in the entire process. Jot down feedback and incorporate it into your hiring process.

TRAINING FOR TEAM EFFECTIVENESS

Building a strong team is never finished, which is why it is one of the five ongoing responsibilities of a leader. Healthy ministries are never static—they grow and expand. Therefore the effectiveness of your team must grow with the ministry. Only one person—the team leader—can ensure this happens.

At ReachGlobal our practice is to determine several important areas of training for our senior teams each year and develop a strategy to carry them out. If you have several key teams in your organization, you will want to ensure that ongoing development is coordinated for all your teams.

One of the most critical areas to help your team develop will be the skills vital to the ministry initiatives you are driving. This ensures alignment between the organization's needs and your team's capacity. One of our organization's recent initiatives was to help all personnel become more intentional in their work through the use of Annual Ministry Plans tied to Key Result Areas. This meant it was critical to train our senior team and then all supervisors how to mentor and coach.

H. I. BEST PRACTICE

Regularly build into your team's agenda major blocks of time for learning together. Keep a list of the training you have done and resources you have used. As new members join your team, ensure there is a plan to "get them up to speed" on issues you have covered so they will be in sync with the rest of the team.

While much team learning will be specific to your organization and the ministry initiatives you are driving, all healthy teams will pay attention to the following areas of training.

Leadership. High-impact teams do a great deal of training in the area of healthy leadership. The more leaders you can develop in your organization the stronger you will be. Necessary skills include how to be a collaborative leader; how to clarify mission, values, preferred future, and ministry initiatives; and the ability to mentor and coach. Some of these issues will be covered later in this book. At the end of this chapter you will find additional resources that can help grow your team's leadership skills.

Sweet spots. Good leaders are exegetes of the people they lead. Too often we simply view people as filling a slot for our organization rather than working to find the best people we can and building their jobs around the gifting and skills God has given them. When people are in a place where they will be successful because the seat was designed for them, they are in their "sweet spots."

H. I. BEST PRACTICE

Find the best people you can and then build their responsibilities around their gifting and wiring so they will be effective and happy in their work. The bottom line is their ability to fulfill the requirements of their areas of responsibility. How they will accomplish the work will depend on their wiring.

If we don't pay attention to people's sweet spots and play to their strengths, team members become frustrated. They are not as productive as if they were situated for maximum effectiveness (and joy) in their work. As a team leader, one of my core missions is to help position the great people on my team in the places where they will be most effective. That means I must watch them, dialogue with them, be willing to modify their job descriptions, and do all I can to keep them engaged.

How do we determine our own (or others') sweet spots? Consider asking these questions:

- What things fill my tank and what things deplete me?
- What things do I love to do and which do I put off?
- What am I most effective at and what am I either marginally effective or really poor at?
- If I could design my perfect job description, what would it be?
- How do others evaluate my strengths and weaknesses?

- If I could change one thing about my current job that would make it a lot more fulfilling, what would it be?

For many years, conventional wisdom said one ought to work on one's weaknesses. We now know it is far wiser to focus on our strengths. In fact, people will be the most productive if they can spend no more than 20 to 40 percent of their time in areas of weakness. We need to help people design their responsibilities in ways that maximize their strengths—and find other ways to support their weaknesses.

If people are really in the wrong spot (they are not playing to their strengths), it may be necessary to help them find another seat on the bus or, if there is not another seat on your bus, a seat on another bus.

Helping your team understand the sweet-spot concept will allow them to apply the same thinking to those they lead.

Emotional intelligence. In the previous chapter we discussed the importance of understanding who we are and our dark sides. We defined Emotional Intelligence (EQ) as the ability to understand ourselves, what drives us, how others perceive us, and how well we relate to others. EQ also affects whether we have the relational skill to work synergistically with others while both being self-defining and allowing others to speak into our lives or work without responding defensively.

Because good EQ plays such an important role in effectiveness of your team and the work of individual members, ongoing discussion and training becomes important. In the church, for instance, more conflict and misunderstandings are caused by poor EQ than by anything else. We cannot expect members of the congregation at large always to display high EQ, but those who are on staff must.

If a team member consistently demonstrates poor EQ—resulting in relational issues—you may need to provide coaching; if that does not work, help him or her find another place to work.

Team dynamics. Remember the definition of *team*: "a group of missionally aligned and healthy individuals working strategically together under good leadership toward common objectives, with accountability for results." This is not possible unless your team works and relates to one another in healthy ways. I defined the characteristics of a healthy team in chapter 1; these areas require ongoing dialogue and training.

Intentional living and ministry. In the next chapter we will look at a paradigm for ensuring those we lead are deeply intentional. On the ministry side, this is a nonnegotiable if one is going to develop high-impact teams and leaders. This intentionality must be a regular topic of discussion because it is easy for teams to revert to activity rather than remain focused on results.

Keeping team members from "leadership default." There is a key principle about teams that is often overlooked and frequently violated: The senior team we serve on is our most important team and is the team of our first allegiance.

This is an important distinction for those of us who both serve on a team and lead a team. I currently serve on the senior team of a denomination. I lead the senior team of that denomination's global ministries. Which team demands my highest loyalty? It is always the senior team I serve on. Why? Because the global-ministry team is under the organizational authority of the senior team. Everything I do with "my" team should align with the senior team. I am first a spokesman for the senior team and second an advocate for the team I lead.

Understanding and living out this principle prevents conflicts between the two teams and ensures organizational alignment. My loyalty to the senior team ensures I lead my team from the perspective of the senior team. I will never allow the team I lead to develop an us/them mentality regarding the senior team, nor will I ever criticize the decisions or direction of the senior denominational team (I helped make the decisions).

Some leaders push back on this position, thinking it limits robust discussion or their ability to deal with issues. Not so. It's a matter of where I deal with the issues. On the senior team, I have all the opportunity in the world to discuss issues that potentially affect my team. That is the correct place for me to air them. Once I leave that room, I become a spokesperson for any decisions made there. With the team I lead, I have an obligation to explain, support, defend, and finesse those decisions so those I lead can understand and work within the parameters of decisions. To not do so is to create deadly divisions that hurt the organization and negatively affect its missional effectiveness.

Let's apply this principle to the church. Senior pastors of most churches serve on the leadership board and also lead a staff team. The leadership board is their senior team that demands their highest loyalty. If senior pastors understand this principle, they will never side with their staff against direction or policies of the board. To do so is to engage in a "leadership default" that fosters an us/them mentality. At the same time, staff members who serve on the senior pastor's team must realize this is *their* senior team. They cannot allow the teams they lead to be at odds with the senior staff team. As leaders, they are always first and foremost spokespersons for that senior staff team.

Neglecting this principle causes no end of conflict between boards and senior staff or between senior staff teams and lower-level ministry teams in a church or organization. It is an authority issue, an alignment issue, and a leadership issue. This does not mean there is not healthy, robust discussion on any team. It does mean the team leaders will not default in their leadership by allowing their teams to be out of alignment with the senior teams they serve on.

Some time ago I met with a team of leaders whose leader serves on my senior team. What I did not realize was that these leaders had a number of questions about the ministry direction we were taking. When they posed their questions to the team leader he would say, "You will have to ask T. J. about that." His response gave the impression that he (a member of my team) was unwilling to take ownership for the direction, even though he was part of all discussions on the decisions we made. In the meeting, his leaders peppered me with questions from a we/you perspective while their leader listened and did not take a position of "I am with T. J. on this, and this is where we are going." My team member had defaulted on leadership, choosing to identify more with the team he led than with the senior team he was on, thus creating an unhealthy situation that allowed an us/them mentality to develop.

Signs of leadership default include the following:

- Siding with your team over or against your senior team—either directly or by implication. This often happens when team leaders feel a need to be popular with those they lead and do not want to take ownership of a decision they were actually a part of.
- Blaming others for decisions your senior team was a part of. For instance, pastors default on leadership when they blame the board for an unpopular decision. As a member of the board they should always own the decision as "ours," not "theirs."
- Not fully supporting and actively defending the senior team's decision or direction with the team one leads.

Leadership default hurts organizations. When we follow the senior-team-first principle, there is alignment within the organization and we are not setting one group against the other or guarding our turf. Living out this principle would prevent most of the us/them mentality of boards against staff, or ministry teams against staff. Those who reject this principle have not learned how to follow well. Those who cannot follow well are not fit to lead.

H. I. BEST PRACTICE

Ensure everyone understands that the senior team they serve on is the team of their first allegiance. If they engage in leadership default, address it quickly. If leadership default becomes a regular practice, define how the behavior hurts the organization and make it clear that it must stop.

THE SPIRITUAL COMPONENT OF HEALTHY MINISTRY TEAMS

This book is written for ministry teams who, by definition, are committed to building Christ's kingdom. Therefore God's wisdom, empowerment, and favor become deeply important in all that we do. As teams in ministry organizations, we must tap into the power of God on a regular basis.

Just as I believe that the spiritual life of church leaders is indispensable to their leadership roles, so I believe that the spiritual life of ministry teams is inseparable from their ability to minister and lead well. As Jesus said of lasting spiritual fruit in John 15:5, "Apart from me you can do nothing." The corollary is that if we remain in Him we will bear much fruit.

Asking the Father to speak into our strategies, give us wisdom, and empower what He places in our hearts is vital to our work as teams. Furthermore, what we model with our team about spiritual dependence will be modeled by our team members in working with those they lead—and will have a cascading effect throughout the organization.

HEALTHY COMMUNICATION IN A "FLAT WORLD"

Communication builds trust, and trust minimizes conflict, because information is power. When it comes to sharing information in an organization, everyone has an opinion, and expectations are hard to meet. Some common complaints I hear are:

- We don't get enough information.
- We get too much information.
- I don't know everything that's happening.
- You did not solicit my opinion or input before you made that decision.
- My leaders don't tell me what is going on.
- Leaders can cascade information down through the organization, but how do I send information back up to them?

These are real issues in the development of healthy organizational cultures and teams. There are some principles that, if understood and practiced, would help address these concerns.

In today's flat world, communication is top down, bottom up, and horizontal—all at once. The day of leaders simply telling the organization what it needs to know are long gone. One of the great blessings of our day is access to information from many sources. Most of us have the ability to communicate quickly throughout the organization to share insights, express opinions, offer solutions, or share challenges. This works both ways. In the traditional top-down organizational structure, employees knew primarily what their leaders wanted to tell them. And, leaders knew primarily what their reports chose to pass back to them. No longer. I can solicit information or receive unsolicited information from anywhere in the organization — and so can anyone else.

Every team member is responsible to share and solicit information. In the old paradigm, it was primarily the job of leaders to communicate pertinent information throughout the organization. In the flat world, it is everyone's job to share information they possess with those who need to know it, regardless of where they fit in the organization.

And we each share the responsibility to solicit the information we need to make the best possible decisions. Rather than fostering a culture of blame (you didn't tell me), we must create cultures of proactive communication in which people at all levels are responsible to each other. This empowers those who practice it because anyone, at any level, can influence the direction of the organization if they are willing to share what they know or solicit what they need to know to do their jobs well.

Organizations that are intentionally healthy create an egalitarian communications culture where everyone has the responsibility and freedom to communicate information. At the same time they retain organizational structure and accountability and support decision making by the right people at the right level.

Not everyone needs to know everything. Small organizations are like families. In families, everyone kind of knows what everyone is kind of doing. It happens naturally. As organizations grow and become more complex, this natural communication is no longer possible. This is a tough transition for those who were in the organization when it was small. Where they always used to be in the know, they no longer are. This is an especially painful shift for staff members in growing churches.

Historically, the organization I lead called itself a family. And, back in the '60s when the denomination was small, it felt like a family. Today it is not a family but an organization; you cannot be "family" with more than five hundred personnel scattered across forty countries. Like a church that has grown out of the family stage, some of our staff who remember the old days still think we are family. When people say to me, "I don't know everything that is happening anymore," I reply, "Neither do I." The truth is, I need to know *certain* things but not a *lot* of things. I expect people to share significant breakthroughs or issues, and always their concerns. But much of what happens I don't know. I am trusting good people to do the right thing. *In a growing organization, anyone who expects to know everything, or even most things, will be disappointed by that unrealistic expectation.*

In a flat organization everyone has responsibility for communication . . .

- To communicate concerns to appropriate people
- To communicate with appropriate parties after decisions are made
- To solicit information from any level of the organization that is needed for making wise decisions
- To alert leadership of barriers, concerns, and opportunities
- To be as transparent as possible on issues that are raised
- To recognize that no one will know everything
- To take personal responsibility for getting information rather than complaining about not receiving it

SUMMARIZING DECISIONS AND ASSIGNMENT

Without someone keeping notes of decisions and assignments, team meetings are sloppy and accountability is difficult. Choose someone on your team who has an administrative gift and give that person the responsibility to record decisions and assignments and send them to all team members immediately after a meeting.

Before you close the meeting, have that person summarize what was recorded to ensure everyone hears the same thing. The "recorder" should then work with the team leader to build the agenda for the next meeting in order to ensure appropriate follow-up on assignments. Remember, execution on missional decisions is what counts.

H. I. BEST PRACTICE

Never end a team meeting without summarizing cascading information, decisions, and assignments. Distribute these to the team immediately after the meeting.

CULTURES OF HEALTHY TEAMS

Every team has rules, written or otherwise, by which it operates. These rules can be healthy or unhealthy. Unhealthy rules might mean certain topics are off limits (the elephants in the room), or they might mean everyone knows nothing can ever be said that the leader could take as critical. Some teams are great at process but do not deal with account-ability or results. Unhealthy rules prevent teams from having candid, honest, robust dialogue.

Only the leader can truly set the tone or culture of a team. Others can try, but the leader has the authority either to encourage or discourage a culture. The more a leader defines the team's "rules of how we work together" and then models that culture, the greater the freedom the team has to operate comfortably with each other. The following rules of engagement would typify a healthy team. It takes healthy Emotional Intelligence on the part of the leader and those on the team to make this possible.

TEAM COVENANT

- We encourage robust dialogue where honest opinions, probing questions, and potential solutions can be freely shared on any topic relating to the team's (or one another's) ministries. We commit to robust dialogue without attacking one another and to maintaining an open, nondefensive attitude.

- In the spirit of Matthew 18, we will always speak in love and keep short accounts when offense has taken place.
- We will regularly evaluate progress of the organization or that part of the organization we are responsible for and do so with utmost honesty. We believe in timely execution and ministry results.
- We practice autopsy without blame. We know things will go wrong. When they do we will analyze the failure so we can learn from it without casting blame for it.
- We keep our promises. When decisions have been made and assignments given, we are committed to executing those assignments fully and on time.
- We take full responsibility for the corporate decisions our team makes and will not engage in leadership default. Our first loyalty is to this team; we will always represent this team well. Outside of our team meetings we speak with one voice.
- We will maintain confidentiality on issues shared in team meetings that should not be shared with others.
- We are committed to thinking the best of one another, speaking the best of one another, praying for one another, and supporting one another's ministries.
- We agree to hold one another accountable for keeping this team covenant, and we agree to allow others to call us on it if we violate this agreement.

H. I. QUESTIONS

For Team Leaders

As you think through those on your team, who are the A-team, B-team, and C-team players?

Are there any team members who either are in the wrong spot or should not be on your team?

What do you need to do differently in choosing team members in the future?

For Team Discussion

What areas could we improve if we were to "do team" better?

Which areas in the team covenant do we practice well? Which do we violate?

What areas of team effectiveness mentioned in this chapter would we like to study together further?

RECOMMENDED READING FOR UNDERSTANDING WHO YOU ARE

Guinness, Os. *The Call: Finding and Fulfilling the Central Purpose of Your Life*. Nashville: Thomas Nelson, 2003.

Kise, Jane A. G., David Stark, and Sandra Krebs Hirsch. *LifeKeys: Discovering Who You Are, Why You're Here, and What You Do Best*. Grand Rapids, MI: Baker, 2005.

Rath, Tom. *StrengthsFinder 2.0: A New and Updated Edition of the Online Test from Gallup's Now, Discover Your Strengths*. New York: Gallup Press, 2007.

Winseman, Albert L., Donald O. Clifton, and Curt Liesveld. *Living Your Strengths: Discover Your God-Given Talents and Inspire Your Community*. New York: Gallup Press, 2004.

RECOMMENDED SELF-KNOWLEDGE TOOLS

Clifton StrengthsFinder
The Clifton StrengthsFinder assessment tool measures a person's talent. This tool is a starting point for self-discovery. *www.strengthsfinder.com*

DiSC
The DiSC Classic Profile tool measures behavioral personality. This assessment provides an understanding of people through increased awareness of temperament and behavioral styles. *www.internalchange.com*

Keirsey Temperament Sorter
The Keirsey Temperament Sorter-II (KTS-II) is a seventy-question personality instrument that helps individuals discover their personality type. *www.advisorteam.org*

Uniquely You Spiritual Gifts Inventory
This tool combines spiritual gifts with the four DiSC personality types. *www.uniquelyyou.com*

CHAPTER SEVEN

THE POWER OF INTENTIONAL LIVING

CHAPTER SUMMARY:

The key distinction of high-impact teams is the intentionality with which leaders and individuals live their lives and pursue their ministries.

People who see significant results of their work think differently from others. They focus on results, not activity. They have chosen intentional living over accidental living.

Key Result Areas (KRAs) help us determine the desired results of our work. They answer the question, "What is success?" They allow us to focus on the critical rather than being driven by the urgent. They help us prioritize and say no to good but noncrucial activities.

Annual Ministry Plans (AMPs) are the specific steps we are going to take to fulfill Key Result Areas. They give us a paradigm for thoughtfully and prayerfully considering what needs to be done and how we will do it. They help us stay on task and measure our progress.

Connecting our Key Result Areas and Annual Ministry Plans to our calendars is "connecting the compass to the clock." It is the linchpin between good planning and good execution.

The key distinction between high-impact teams and other teams is the intentionality with which leaders and individuals live and pursue ministry. We live in a day of huge needs, multiplied demands, out-of-control schedules, and the tendency to be driven by the urgent. Over time, our effectiveness is eroded and our hearts grow tired. We know deep down that there must be a better way to live life and pursue ministry.

Three observations ought to give us pause. First, we are all busy. When people describe to me how busy they are and how fast they run in ministry, I am not impressed; we're all busy.

Second, we are all busy, but not everyone sees the same results. Some people are exceedingly productive while others accomplish little.

Third, activity does not equal results. This is a critical distinction. That is why I am unimpressed with how packed one's schedule is. The question is not how much activity we are involved in, but what the results are. Activity that is not strategic yields little for the energy expended and leaks away opportunity for kingdom results.

People who see significant results of their work think differently from others. Rather than focusing on activity, they focus on results. They have identified the results they want to see for their lives and then strategically focused their activity toward those results. They are highly discriminating in what they do, the obligations they agree to, and how they schedule their days. Before they say yes to new opportunities they think and pray, determine whether the activity will contribute to what they understand to be the critical issues of their lives, and practice the power of saying no.

H. I. DEFINITION

Intentional living is the discipline of knowing how God made you, defining the top issues in your life and work, and executing with an intentional annual plan that connects your schedule with your priorities in a way that maximizes your God-given gifting and call.

ACCIDENTAL AND INTENTIONAL LIVING

All of us live somewhere on a continuum between accidental and intentional living. I have contrasted the difference as follows. Look carefully at the column on the left and then the column on the right.

|---Accidental Living---Intentional Living---|

• Lives moment by moment	• Lives within structure
• Often harried	• Seldom harried
• Little advanced planning	• Significant advanced planning
• Does not distinguish between "big rocks" and "small rocks"	• Distinguishes between critical and noncritical
• Busy without well-defined priorities	• Schedule revolves around key priorities
• Allows life to determine schedule	• Mission drives schedule

H. I. MOMENT

Mark those characteristics just listed that best describe how you live. Do you fall more on the accidental or the intentional side of the continuum? Are you pleased with where you are?

How intentionally we live matters. From a personal perspective, the issue is whether we are using the gifts, time, and opportunities Christ has given us to the fullest advantage. We have one life to live and it goes fast. On the other side of fifty, I am on the downslope of opportunity, timewise, but have a greater ability to influence others given my stage of life and the lessons I have learned.

I meet few individuals who want to squander their lives, yet the way they go about life does not match their desires. Lack of careful thinking about priorities and schedules, and not living in light of the gifts and opportunities God has given us, equals living accidentally.

In John 15, Jesus makes it clear that fruit matters to God. Our lives are not only to bear fruit but to bear "much fruit," fruit that will last. Producing this fruit is directly related to how intentionally we live our lives. The fruit of our lives will be congruent with the gifting God has given us and the work that he "prepared in advance for us to do"

(Ephesians 2:10). All things being equal, the choices we make are the crucial difference between those who accomplish much and those who accomplish little.

High-impact leaders and teams are made up of people who refuse to settle for out-of-control schedules, unfocused activity, and meeting the expectations of others. Rather, they are deeply thoughtful about what God has called them to accomplish, focusing strategic activity on the critical areas. This intentionality comes out of a deep sense of God's call and their stewardship of that call.

OVERWHELMING DESIRES AND UNDERWHELMING PLANS

No one reading this book wants to squander opportunities to influence our world for Christ. We have an overwhelming desire for significance. But many of us have an underwhelming plan for how to satisfy that desire!

Unless we develop an intentional plan and a sustained life rhythm we will not fulfill our desire for lives of significance. Let's face it, accidental living is an easy default position because it takes no discipline. Intentional living demands a price. The price includes doing the hard work of understanding what God has called us to accomplish and how we are wired, along with the discipline to focus our activity toward those critical issues that spell success for our lives and work. Those who do the hard work and live their lives with discipline see far more fruit than those who don't.

High-impact teams insist all members live (at least in the workplace) with a huge degree of intentionality. They focus on results, strategic activity, and a rhythm that keeps everyone aligned with one another and the mission of the team. It is a deeply satisfying place to be.

LEGACY

Fast-forward to the day of your funeral. Your family is there, as well as your friends and colleagues. What are they saying about your life? What are your children remembering? Your spouse? Those who knew you best? If there were a handful of things you would want to be remembered for, what would they be?

H. I. MOMENT

At the end of my life I would want people to remember me for:

_____

_____

_____

_____

Assume you have five years left in your current ministry. If you could accomplish three to five things that leave a lasting influence, what would they be?

1. _____
2. _____
3. _____
4. _____
5. _____

You have just identified your "big rocks." They are the key results you want from your life and work. In a pile of rocks of different sizes, the smaller rocks, pebbles, and grains of sand sift to the bottom. The pebbles and grains of sand are important, but they aren't the top issues. Getting these big rocks right is one of the most important things you can do if you are going to live intentionally. Answer this question for each of the big rocks you listed above: How strategically is my activity aligned with this key result? Be honest with yourself.

1. _____
2. _____
3. _____
4. _____
5. _____

KEY RESULT AREAS

Understanding of and commitment to Key Result Areas (KRAs) is a major contributor in moving from mere activity to focused living. Much of what we have seen modeled or been taught about structuring our lives focuses on activity. For instance, most job descriptions list the activities the job entails. The message is that if one carries out those activities one will be successful in the work. But it is not true!

A major fallacy is in operation here, because activity does not equal results. Many people's work lives are filled with activity with not much to show for it. The key to intentional living is identifying what the *results* of our work ought to be rather than the *activity* the job entails. That was the point of the exercises you just completed.

KRAs help us determine the desired results of our work. They answer the question of success and are applicable in both our personal and professional lives. KRAs do not define activity, goals, or methods; they define the ultimate outcome we want to see in any given year.

H. I. DEFINITION

Key Result Areas (KRAs) are the specific results that spell success in our jobs and lives. KRAs describe success (results), not how we will achieve results (activity). KRAs define the critical results one must achieve if one is going to be successful in one's work.

Because KRAs define what success looks like, they cut through the clutter of activity and get to the heart of the matter: what our activity must *lead* to. Key Result Areas allow us to focus on the critical rather than be driven by the urgent. They clarify our nonnegotiable priorities and move us to allocate our time and energy based on a set of clear outcomes that will allow us to fulfill God's call on our lives.

Think of all the demands on us. All of us have options and opportunities as to what we could do with our time; we also face regular pressures to fulfill others' expectations—people love to tell us what is important and how we should spend our time. Every day we face questions:

- How do we prioritize?
- How do we schedule?
- What gives us the confidence to say yes or no?
- Where do we focus?
- How do we deal with competing voices?
- How do we free ourselves from the tyranny of the urgent?

The answer is to identify Key Result Areas. They become the grid from which you can answer these questions.

Five nonnegotiable KRAs for every leader. Think back to the priorities of a leader spelled out in chapter 5. These are the Key Result Areas that spell success for team leaders:

1. *Personal development*—Ensuring they live intentionally in their spiritual, emotional, relational, and professional life
2. *Strategic leadership*—Providing strategic leadership to the organization or the part of the organization they lead
3. *Strong team*—Building a healthy, unified, aligned, strategic, and results-oriented team
4. *Leadership development*—Developing current and future leaders
5. *Mobilizing resources*—Mobilizing resources necessary for the team's ministry to flourish

Note that these KRAs do not spell out methods or strategies; rather, they define the end result. If team leaders can successfully keep their lives on track, provide the right strategic leadership, build a strong and healthy team, develop current and future leaders, and mobilize needed resources, they will be successful. They may have additional Key Result Areas, but these five are nonnegotiable for those who lead teams.

H. I. MOMENT

Think through the Key Result Areas that would spell success in your job. Answer the question, "What things do I need to accomplish to successfully do my job?" Do not include methodology or action steps.

1. _____
2. _____
3. _____
4. _____
5. _____

Share your conclusions with other members of your team and invite their input. Do they agree that this is what success would look like for you?

KRAs help us prioritize. Once we understand our Key Result Areas, they become the grid through which we can measure demands and opportunities. In my role, I have many opportunities to attend far-flung meetings, to speak, or to be on various boards. I also have many people who would like to determine my priorities — in a way that aligns with theirs! It would be easy to say yes to good but nonessential activities, either because I enjoy doing them (the meeting was in Greece after all!) or because I feel pressured to accept. How do I determine whether to say yes or no? By my KRAs! For example, does the meeting help me build a strong team or mobilize resources? As I say to my team, "There are lots of things I could do as your leader, but if I do not accomplish these things (my KRAs), the organization will suffer and I will have failed as a leader." My KRAs provide an extraordinary amount of clarity regarding my priorities. And these priorities take precedence over everything else.

THE POWER OF NO

There is an interesting passage about Jesus in Mark 1. Jesus was in Capernaum, where he healed Simon's mother-in-law and "many who had various diseases. He also drove out many demons" (verse 34). Early the next morning Jesus went to a quiet place to pray. When Simon and his companions found Jesus, they told Him, "Everyone is looking for you!" (verse 37).

Jesus' response is surprising. Rather than do what the disciples expected and respond to those looking for Him, He replied, "Let us go somewhere else—to the nearby villages—so I can preach there also" (verse 38). He said no to the need and expectation the disciples brought to Him because He had more important missional things to do. Jesus understood the power of no. He could distinguish between those things that were *good* and those things that were *critical* for His ministry.

It should not be lost on us that Jesus said no to the disciples' expectation *after* He had spent time with His Father. Jesus was in the habit of taking time to refresh His intimacy with the Father and to pray through what He should be doing so His priorities were aligned with His Father's.

We can learn from Jesus' "no" to the disciples. Most of us love to please others. Saying yes makes others feel good about us—and we feel good about ourselves. We get our cookies by pleasing people!

I once did a consultation with a senior pastor of a large church. I was there because his staff felt he did not pay enough attention to them and to building a strong team. When I probed the pastor about how he spent his time (activities), I learned he made all the hospital calls—in a large church! When I asked why, he said, "Because it makes me feel good." At least he was honest. While his activity was good, it was not focused on his true big rocks, which included building a strong staff team (results). His team suffered because he focused on the wrong activity—for him.

Yes and *no* are powerful words with powerful results. Saying yes to the right things allows us to focus on the areas that spell success for us. Saying no to nice but not strategic activity is equally powerful. God has called each of us to a few Key Result Areas, and lots of good and nice activities seek to distract us from those areas. Wise people refuse to be sidetracked by the nice at the expense of the important.

Saying no is not easy. When I am asked to consider an opportunity, my usual answer is, "I will think and pray about it and get back to you." I rarely agree on the spot. Often I consult a trusted colleague for a second opinion on whether the opportunity is truly important. After thinking, praying, and considering my schedule and Key Result Areas, I accept or decline. I am learning that "no" can be a very powerful tool in accomplishing what God has called me to do. I cannot say yes to those things without saying no to other good things.

KRAS AND SWEET SPOTS

In chapter 6, we discussed "sweet spots"—the importance of ensuring we spend 60 to 80 percent of our time ministering out of our strengths. Staying in our sweet spots is key to success with KRAs because God wired us the way He wired us for a purpose. Only when we are working in line with our gifting will we be happy and productive.

A word to those who are just starting out in ministry. You may not yet have clarity on your strengths (although the testing we have suggested can help). Time has a way of helping us understand ourselves, so pay attention to where you are and are not strong when trying different things. As you do so, you will start to discern your strengths.

I indicated that trying to make weaknesses into strengths is not a good strategy—because it just won't happen. So how do we deal with weaknesses? One reason for ministering with a team is that there is a good chance someone on your team is strong where you are weak. I have a "support system" for areas where I know I'm no good and need others to help. Look around your team for someone who can pick up where you are weak. If there is nobody, go find someone! Or consider the option to just stop doing what you are not good at. Sometimes that is the best choice—as long as it is not a critical part of your role.

If you feel you are totally out of your area of strengths, don't ignore that. Trying to do a job that is not within your core strength areas will be deeply frustrating. Your frustration will spill over to others, and you will not be the productive person God made you to be. Be intentional in finding a job that suits you better.

High-impact leaders have a significant responsibility to ensure those who report to them are ministering out of their strengths. To do otherwise is to set up people to fail and to compromise your mission.

ANNUAL MINISTRY PLANS

Key Result Areas do not necessarily change from year to year unless the focus of one's job changes. What does change are the Annual Ministry Plans (AMPs), which describe *how* one is going to fulfill each Key Result Area in a given year. Intentionality is about understanding the end goal (KRAs) and how one can best get there (AMPs).

H. I. DEFINITION

Annual Ministry Plans (AMPs) are the specific steps one is going to take in any given year to fulfill one's KRAs.

Before the beginning of a year (whether a calendar year or a ministry year), all team members should have determined their KRAs and AMPs—the specific plans they intend to drive to fulfill those KRAs. These plans are developed by the individuals and then endorsed by their supervisors (at the end of the chapter, you'll see a sample of my KRAs and AMPs for a year, as well as sample KRAs and AMPs from a team member).

AMPs ensure good planning. While the secular world has long stressed such planning, the ministry world has been significantly behind, especially when it comes to focusing on results. Good ministry is impossible without good planning. At the heart of intentionality is a commitment to prayerfully think through what needs to be done and how one should do it. This may be a stretch for people who are not used to planning, but they will get used to it and their work results will be measurably better.

KRAs and AMPs provide for both empowerment and accountability. In the absence of KRAs or AMPs it is difficult for managers to avoid controlling or micromanaging. After all, they don't know what team members might be doing. In order to empower, one has to clearly define the expectations through KRAs and AMPs. Then there can be a monthly mentoring/coaching checkup driven by the AMPs.

AMPs help measure progress. Monthly mentoring/coaching meetings between supervisors and team members can use this plan to gauge progress. Because team members developed the plan themselves (with supervisor sign-off), they can be held accountable for its execution.

For team members, AMPs provide the road map for the year in terms of what they need to concentrate on. The hard part—knowing what to do—is past and now they can concentrate on executing the plan. AMPs are a wonderfully helpful tool for self-management. It puts the responsibility for ministry execution on individual team members rather than on the team leader.

There are people in the ministry world who believe results do not really matter. I am told on occasion that "the only thing that matters is faithfulness." While faithfulness is a nonnegotiable, results do matter—because they matter to God. We are all about "much fruit" (John 15:5). AMPs help us measure how much progress we are making according to the plans we have laid out.

AMPs form the basis for annual reviews. The ministry world is notoriously lax in helping people know the success of their performances. KRAs and AMPs make an objective annual performance review possible. How did the team member do in fulfilling his or her AMPs and therefore KRAs? Even if not executed perfectly (intentionality, not perfection is the goal), the presence of a plan makes evaluation easier and forms the basis of the next year's AMPs.

CONNECTING THE COMPASS TO THE CLOCK

The world is filled with good intentions. And that is all KRAs and AMPs are unless they are connected to how we use our time. Once we have defined success, the most critical element in living intentionally is to actually connect our intentions with our schedules.

Apart from Scripture, no document is more important to us than our schedules. Time is the one asset we cannot get back. How we spend our time (activity) has a direct impact on the results of our life and work (success). High-impact teams do not live by the seat of their pants or on the fly. Many people do, but high-impact people do not. And high-impact leaders do not allow team members to settle for accidental living.

I often ask my senior leaders to share their schedules with me. I can tell from looking at their schedules what my leaders' true priorities are. My own schedule is available to all my key leaders — they can look any time they choose. It is my way of setting an example of how I connect the compass to the clock, and it makes me accountable to those I hold accountable. I cannot ask of others what I do not practice myself.

Schedule your priorities. Either we schedule time in our month to work on our AMPs, or life and others will schedule us instead. A simple way to be intentional about your KRAs and AMPs is to schedule your week with blocks of time carved out for your priorities. Blocks of time allow you to focus on specific aspects of your annual plan. Once you have scheduled your priorities, you can fill in the rest of the schedule with the meetings, administration, and other activities that are part of your life.

I color code my schedule so I can track where I am spending my time and determine at a glance whether I am giving adequate time to my five KRAs.

As you schedule your priorities, think about the time of day you will be most productive for a specific task. I do much better in the morning with focused blocks of time (I started writing this morning at four o'clock). For me, afternoons are better spent in meetings, answering e-mail, and taking care of administrative tasks.

Do not allow administrative duties to take precedence over activities that will drive your AMPs and KRAs. Even senior leaders can be fooled into thinking they are using their time strategically when they are not. Unless our time use connects directly to accomplishing our mission and KRAs, we are confusing activity with results.

Control your interruptions. Focused individuals develop tools to control interruptions. There are blocks of time when the phone should not be answered, when e-mail should not be read, and when we are not accessible to others (except in emergencies). Most of us are good at keeping appointments we have with other people. My approach is that an appointment for focused work is as sacred as an appointment with a person. I work hard to keep them both.

We know that life interrupts, so leaving margin in one's schedule allows flexibility when one must adjust, which should happen seldomly. Remember, either we control our schedules or others will do it for us. We make the choice as to how intentional and disciplined we will be with the most important asset we have—our time.

Schedule thinking, reading, and planning time. A secret of high-impact leaders is that they block out time to think, read, and plan. They put into their schedule specific days or even weeks when they will be out of the office, away from distractions. When we give our minds the opportunity, we will connect dots about our lives and ministries in ways that can revolutionize our effectiveness, strategy, or paradigms. If you are a visual person, use a whiteboard or journal to jot down ideas or sketch out diagrams. With time, these thoughts will marinate until you come to clarity. The key is giving our minds the opportunity. Effective people take the time to think—intentionally. Schedule it in!

Don't do what others can do. Some things only you can do. But there are many things others can do as well or better than you. Delegate those things you do not need to do. This allows you to focus on what you must do and on the priorities you have determined by KRAs and AMPs. Every year I ask, "What can I give away to others so I can focus more directly on the most important things I must do?" This allows me to "up my game" and be more effective as a leader.

H. I. BEST PRACTICE

Think through your schedule and make a list of all the activities someone else could do. If it is not critical for you to do, and someone else can do it at least 70 percent as well as you can, give it away. By doing so you "up your game" and you empower others.

Build in accountability for schedules. Because connecting the compass to the clock is so critical, I strongly suggest that team members be asked to show their team leader their schedules during their monthly mentoring/

coaching meeting (see chapter 8). This is not to control but to build in accountability for how team members spend time and to give the leader opportunity to coach team members about how to be more strategic in time management.

If your team uses common scheduling software, make calendar sharing a standard practice and ask team members to be specific about what is on their calendars. There is great peer accountability with transparency about how people use their time. Leaders set the pace by their own discipline and being open about what they are up to. Trust is also generated when others know what you are doing.

H. I. BEST PRACTICE

Make all calendars available to supervisors, peers, and team members.

Identify your top three priorities each month. None of us can concentrate on everything. On a monthly basis, identify the top three priorities you are going to concentrate on. These should be directly connected to your KRAs and AMPs. Report these priorities to your supervisor along with your results from last month's top three priorities.

Foster a culture of execution and results. Execution, the discipline of getting things done, is a focus of high-impact teams. As teams meet, or as supervisors and team members meet for coaching/mentoring meetings, the discussion should always include results. By focusing on real results aligned with the organization's mission and on team members' KRAs, we send a strong message that our work is not about activity but results. Many ministries do not have a culture of results.

When one reads the New Testament, there is a major focus on results. Think of Paul's many admonitions regarding how we live our lives so we run the race well and are worthy of the prize. The book of Acts stresses the fruit (results) of the early church, including the number of people who were added. Jesus emphasized the results of changed lives in those who claimed to follow Him. He said that if we stay connected with the vine we will see much fruit (results) in our lives. Paul's mission to Ephesus described in Acts 19 resulted in the whole region being influenced with the gospel (results).

Because we are missional in our thinking, we are always seeking the most God-honoring results of our activity. Foster that kind of culture, and your organization will be better for it.

PERSONAL RETREAT DAYS

A large part of helping your team be successful is to ensure they stay in alignment with their KRAs and AMPs. A monthly personal retreat day outside the office facilitates this alignment. During this day, team members plan and evaluate life and work against the KRAs and AMPs they have adopted for the year. Personal retreat days follow the example of Christ, who regularly went off by Himself to spend time with the Father in prayer and meditation.

The purpose of the day is to:

- Review KRAs and AMPs
- Make necessary adjustments where you are out of alignment
- Determine the top three priorities for the coming month
- Review the top three priorities of the prior month
- Think and pray about upcoming obligations. This includes considering possible engagements you have not decided on in light of your KRA priorities. Spend time in prayer asking for wisdom and guidance
- Perhaps spend time in a key personal or work-related book
- Write your monthly prayer update to your personal prayer team

H. I. DEFINITION

Personal retreat days are a monthly day reserved on the calendar and set aside for planning, thinking, prayer, review of KRAs and AMPs, and writing a monthly prayer letter. They are best done off-site, without other appointments or interruptions.

When I teach on intentional living, people will often respond to the concept of a personal retreat day with, "I don't have time to do that." My response is, "You don't have time not to do that." Intentionality is the key to living productively instead of simply experiencing endless activity. The more carefully we think through priorities, the more productive we will be. It is amazing what happens when we take the time to stop and think and pray. It is perhaps the most important work we do because it is the key to effective work.

PERSONAL PRAYER TEAMS

Some years ago, a dear friend gave me the greatest gift anyone could give. He volunteered to set up a personal prayer team for me and my family. He brought together a number of couples from around the country who loved us, were committed to us, and were trustworthy. They formed an inner, core prayer team that has sustained us over many years.

We feel free to share anything going on in our lives with this inner, core team—whether marriage, family, work, or other issues. We communicate with them at least monthly, sometimes more. They are committed to complete confidentiality, and we are committed to being transparent. They have sustained us through dark days and bright ones.

We also have a second, larger prayer team of several hundred people. I typically send them a monthly update with a short report of the past month, my calendar for the current month, as well as any special requests we have as a family. I am convinced that any success I see in my job is a direct result of the prayers of these dear partners. How grateful I am that they have faithfully upheld me, our ministry, my wife and her ministry, and our two boys.

High-impact ministry is not possible without regular intercession. As Paul indicated, we are involved in a spiritual battle that requires spiritual weapons (see Ephesians 6). The more intercession we have, the more protection we have. I, for one, want all the protection and power I can appropriate!

Because the personal retreat day is for evaluation, planning, alignment, and prayer, it is a great time to update prayer teams for the coming month. Not only are we touching base with our priorities and plans, but we also are touching base with our Lord and those who uphold us before the throne.

H. I. BEST PRACTICE

Develop two prayer groups to uphold you, your family, and your ministry. First seek an inner, core group with whom you can be completely transparent regarding issues you are facing. This requires a commitment to confidentiality on their part and transparency on yours. Then form a larger, outer group and keep them updated monthly on issues for which you would like prayer.

ANNUAL PLANNING RETREATS

If planning is the key to intentionality, then an annual planning retreat for all key ministry personnel must be part of their jobs and rhythms. I recommend at least a three-day personal retreat for planning, prayer, and finalization of the next year's annual ministry plan. As I indicated previously, KRAs will often not change unless the focus of one's job has changed. However, AMPs will change, since the coming year builds on the previous year.

Following this planning retreat, two additional steps are necessary. First, a meeting with one's supervisor should be scheduled to review AMPs and ensure the supervisor is in agreement, since this plan will form the basis of monthly meetings and the annual review. Second, it is helpful for team members to share plans with each other to ensure alignment among all the members' plans and efforts.

If your team is working from team KRAs, it is important to define them before individuals develop their individual plans, so their KRAs and AMPs support those of the team.

NEVER NEGLECT THE SOURCE

Proverbs 4:23 says, "Above all else, guard your heart, for it is the well-spring of life." As Christ followers involved in kingdom work, this is the single most foundational principle for living intentionally. We choose to guard our hearts because their passions, contents, desires, and purity influence our decisions, priorities, and kingdom impact. What we do with our hearts affects everything about who we are and where we are able to lead others.

Choosing to be intentional and proactive in growing our relationship with Christ is the single most important decision we can make. Intentionality means regular, not haphazard; planned into our schedules, not an afterthought; a priority, not ancillary. Realizing that we connect with God and grow in different ways, my goal is not to prescribe how you do this but to challenge you to give it a high priority. I practice what I call "unhurried time with God" when I pray, listen, and meditate.

There are three reasons this time with Christ is so critical. The first is that, according to Jesus, our lives are simply an overflow of our hearts (see Matthew 7:15-20). Think on that for a moment. The more we immerse ourselves in Christ, the more our lives will overflow with His content. This overflow is an unconscious result of living in His presence. One cannot manufacture it; it is either there or not.

Second, as people who are in ministry, we need wisdom and insight into strategies, people, situations, and problems. Who has that insight? The closer we are to Christ, the more "audibles" we will hear where God drops ideas, information, or answers into our hearts, and we say, "That's it!" All of us have probably had that happen. God is heard most easily by listening ears and open hearts; those senses are tuned by spending time with Him.

Third, we are in the business of leading others closer to Him. We can lead people only where we have already gone. The closer we stay to Him, the better we can lead people to Him.

H. I. MOMENT

How well are you doing in guarding your heart? Very well, average, or marginal?

Do you have an intentional and proactive plan to stay close to Christ that makes this a high priority in your schedule? Do you need to revisit this area of life so you are more intentional?

LIVING WITH INTENTIONALITY

Good leaders and high-impact teams choose to live and work with great intentionality and accountability. With our KRAs and AMPs, we have a road map for our year. We may have to adjust to circumstances, but we can self-manage for maximum results rather than settling for activity and hoping for results. In addition, because our supervisors have endorsed our KRAs and AMPs, there is no need for them to manage us, nor do we need to manage those who report to us, other than to ensure they stay focused on their KRAs and AMPs.

Key Result Areas and Annual Ministry Plans foster a culture of empowerment because once the KRAs are defined, team members have a great amount of freedom to determine their AMPs and the strategy they will employ to meet their KRAs. Leaders and supervisors become encouragers, coaches, consultants, and equippers rather than primarily managers and directors.

Having maximum clarity around one's KRAs allows one to:

- Develop an annual plan around those priorities
- Choose opportunities based on KRAs
- Say no or yes with freedom
- Differentiate between competing voices and agendas
- Delegate areas that are not one's prime responsibility
- Stay focused on the main thing for one's life

KRAs should be within our sweet spots and reflect what we believe God's call on our lives to be. Having determined them and having the agreement of our supervisors, we have the freedom to focus on those few areas that both become our priorities and spell success in our jobs and lives.

H. I. QUESTIONS FOR TEAM LEADERS

On a scale of 1 to 10, with 10 being deeply intentional, where would you place yourself on the intentionality scale?_____

What is the hardest discipline for you in regard to intentionality?

How do you see the connection between God-given opportunity, life call, and intentionality?

Is there currently a good connection between your top priorities and your sweet spot? Explain.

What things do you do that you could have others do?

Do you find it easy or difficult to say no to expectations that do not fit your priorities? Why?

SAMPLE 1: KRAS AND AMPS OF AN ORGANIZATIONAL LEADER

KRA One: Personal Development
Summary: Ensure I live intentionally in my spiritual, family, and professional life.

> *Goal:* Stay on track with Jesus.
> *Plan:* Daily unhurried time with Christ, read through
> the Scriptures, practice a monthly retreat day,
> keep a journal, communicate with prayer teams
> monthly.

> *Goal:* Stay focused.
> *Plan:* Monthly retreat day, annual retreat, prioritize
> schedule according to KRAs, delegate issues that
> can be delegated.

Goal: Keep marriage vital.
Plan: Weekly date with Mary Ann when home, pray
      regularly together, keep her current with my
      work, travel together when possible.

Goal: Be engaged as a dad.
Plan: Find ways to connect with Jon and Steven, pray
      regularly for them, always be available to them.

Goal: Grow my leadership quotient.
Plan: Read and think regularly on leadership and
      missions, develop relationships with other mission
      leaders, continue to write for the church, leaders,
      and ReachGlobal staff.

Goal: Be accountable.
Plan: Invite accountability and input from a key group
      of friends and the ReachGlobal board, be
      transparent with staff on schedules and priorities,
      keep my prayer team aware of needs and schedule.

KRA Two: Strategic Leadership

Summary: Provide strategic leadership to ReachGlobal (RG) values, mission, and vision for the future through annual strategic initiatives.

- Review and finalize all current key documents of RG to ensure a common voice and proper alignment.
- Drive intentional diversity in RG domestically and internationally.
- Help RG move toward greater multiplication in all of our ministries.
- Champion the RG sandbox.
- Provide maximum clarity to leadership and personnel.
- Provide regular communication to personnel re: vision, opportunity, and strategy.

- Realign schedule for less activity and more "think time."
- Ensure benchmarking of new metrics.
- Develop relationships with national movement leaders.

KRA Three: Strong Team

Summary: Build a strong, unified, aligned, strategic, and results-oriented team to lead ReachGlobal.

- Design March and November meetings that are venues for networking, training, encouraging, and missional alignment.
- Spend time with Directional Leaders to encourage, coach, and be aware of their ministry world and needs.
- Model the leadership qualities and commitments we have articulated for all RG leaders.
- Over the next twenty-four months, ensure all RG personnel are trained in the concepts of leading from the sandbox.

KRA Four: Leadership Development

Summary: Develop current and future leaders of ReachGlobal and influence national partners.

- Ensure the intentional development of the Lead Team through annual events, clusters, and communication.
- Ensure the completion of the Leadership Pipeline with job descriptions, competencies, and training necessary for each level; ensure training of leaders consistent with the Pipeline.
- Ensure that leaders are mentor coaches, that RG personnel receive monthly coaching/mentoring from supervisors, and that all individuals and teams are using KRAs and AMPs.
- Implement intentional personal mentoring of ten individuals at various levels in the EFCA to develop the next generation of leaders.
- Ensure leaders are identifying and mentoring potential leaders in RG regardless of the level in which they currently work.

KRA Five: Mobilization of Resources

Summary: Mobilize key resources necessary for ReachGlobal to flourish and build for the future.

- Keep prayer initiatives in front of leaders and staff.
- Ensure GVP hits its financial goal this year; raise new resources for the International Leadership fund and other strategic projects for RG.
- Identify and challenge leaders within and outside EFCA movement to consider joining RG in leadership roles.
- Ensure regular communication with mission pastors and mission committee members via a broadcast e-mail and Sandcastles.

SAMPLE 2: KRAS AND AMPS OF A TEAM MEMBER

Big Rocks for This Year:

1. Coordinate and launch new EFCA website.
2. Transition to/acquire new responsibilities.
3. Focus on multiplication in admin processes/procedures.

KRA One: Personal Development

Summary: Focus on holistic health and growth including spiritual, relational, and physical health.

1. Grow in spiritual health and in relationship with God.
   a. Take monthly personal retreat day.
   b. Take on one new responsibility at church.
   c. Memorize two ten-verse sections of the Bible.
   d. Read one book on faith.
   e. Spend time in the Word at least once a week for twenty-plus minutes.
   f. Pray daily for marriage, family, and work.

2. Grow in relational health.
   a. Spend intentional quality time alone with my husband each week.
   b. Spend intentional quality time with my son each day.
   c. Talk with my sisters at least two to three times per week.
   d. Talk with my family members once per week.
   e. Spend time with one other couple at least once per week.

3. Focus on optimal physical health.
   a. Get at least seven hours of sleep a day.
   b. Spend thirty-plus minutes, at least three days a week, in an aerobic workout.
   c. Limit to two sodas/coffees per week—always decaf.
   d. Train for a triathlon.

KRA Two: Strategic Leadership

Summary: Give strategic leadership to administrative support staff and strategic ReachGlobal initiatives.

1. Align administrative support staff with mission/vision of EFCA ReachGlobal.
   a. Meet monthly with team to inform them of leadership decisions, initiatives, etc.
   b. Review sandbox once a year.
   c. Develop KRAs for admin team.
   d. Meet monthly with direct reports.
   e. Assess administrative processes to ensure multiplication.

2. Lead ReachGlobal staff through new strategic initiatives.
   a. Launch new website in October.
      1. Work with ministry leaders to assess needs.
      2. Elicit and coordinate up-to-date content.
      3. Be primary communicator to staff regarding new site.
      4. Coordinate with and activate divisions to use new site; train others to manage/filter information.

    b.   Oversee communication developments/publications.

       1. Be primary communicator to staff regarding publications.

       2. Work with admin staff in execution of publications.

       3. Assess communication needs and work with director to create solutions.

KRA Three: Strong Team

Summary: Focus on building a team that is unified, motivated, and proactive in supporting the mission of the EFCA and ReachGlobal.

1. Meet regularly with admin staff team.
   - a. Schedule a monthly team meeting.
   - b. Set up monthly coaching/mentoring meeting with direct reports.
   - c. Affirm behavior that is proactive, positive, motivated, and missional.
   - d. Help team function as a network that understands other members' work.

2. Focus on team building and community.
   - a. Develop admin staff.
   - b. Schedule at least one admin team retreat day annually.
   - c. Do a team-building exercise quarterly during our monthly meetings.

3. Focus on transition.
   - a. Train/mentor another person to succeed in my responsibilities as team leader.
   - b. Pursue additional challenges and responsibilities in team leader roles.

KRA Four: Staff/Individual Development

Summary: Focus on effectively developing staff and individuals both inside and outside of ReachGlobal.

1. Offer ongoing training.
   a. Facilitate and advocate ongoing training for administrative support staff.
   b. Provide project training.
   c. Provide new website training.
   d. Provide skills-based training opportunities (job specific).

2. Meet with admin staff regularly.
   a. Schedule monthly mentoring meetings with staff.
   b. Continue to help facilitate goals for development in their jobs.
   c. Ensure their processes support multiplication.
   d. Schedule monthly team meetings.
   e. Advocate ongoing training.
   f. Host trainings for the teams to experience together.
   g. Ask questions about needed skills/training. Follow through with opportunities.

3. Develop myself as a leader.
   a. Attend at least one conference that provides leadership training.
   b. Pursue additional leadership responsibilities in and/or outside of ReachGlobal.
   c. Meet with leadership mentors once per month.

KRA Five: Mobilization of Resources

Summary: Assist in acquiring and wisely distributing resources for maximum ministry effectiveness in ReachGlobal.

1. Administrate and oversee EFCA EQUIP sites for the following teams: Board site, Directional Team site, Lead Team site, Internal site.

2. Oversee ReachGlobal publications.
   a. Oversee content of publications and submissions.

  b. Ensure information is readily available to ReachGlobal and EFCA staff.

  c. Ensure content is mission critical to the ministry of the respective audience.

3. Mobilize materials that support the ministry of our personnel.

  a. Update personnel regularly with available resources. Respond to requests for material within twenty-four hours.

  b. Assess materials necessary for effective ministry and assist in providing solutions.

4. Mobilize information and resources to assist the executive director.

  a. Respond to the executive director's request for info within twenty-four hours.

  b. Anticipate information and resource needs before they arise and communicate to the executive director.

  c. Write drafts or documents on behalf of the executive director.

  d. Participate in directional team meetings and disseminate necessary information throughout the organization.

CHAPTER EIGHT

BECOMING A MENTOR/COACH

CHAPTER SUMMARY:

Good team members do not want to be "managed" or controlled, but released to become the best they can be. Great leaders desire the same for their teams and take an intentional posture of a mentor/coach.

Coaches love to release the gifting and potential in others by making meaningful time for the people who report to them. They probe, ask questions, and help their people think well and come to healthy conclusions. They care about their people as a whole, help them find their sweet spots for maximum joy and effectiveness, and hold them with an open hand. They want the very best for those they coach.

Mentors give honest and direct feedback so their people are clear on areas where their performance is great and where it is problematic. They practice a "no surprises" policy and provide help when performance or EQ are substandard.

Mentor/coaches use carefully crafted monthly meetings to ensure their people stay on track — in line with their KRAs and AMPs. This allows good people to flourish and eliminates the need for micromanagement. Annual evaluations bring no surprises as honest feedback takes place on a monthly basis.

Good leaders use the mentor/coach paradigm to build great teams, develop their people, and keep them aligned. They make the tough calls to remove ineffective people when necessary so the mission is never compromised.

Great leaders love to develop great people, and they make it a priority!

What does it mean to be a supervisor?

For many the word *manager* comes to mind. But think about that. Do you like to be "managed"? That word often connotes control; it says that my manager does not trust me to do the job I have been hired to do or that two people need to have a hand in doing my job—my manager and me. Controlling supervisors seldom develop high-impact teams because the best people will not sign on. Or, if they do sign on, they don't stay.

Do you really want to "manage" others? Most ministry leaders and supervisors I know find the job frustrating and time-consuming. And it should be, because good people were not made to be managed. They were made to be empowered, set free, and then coached and mentored. If the people on your team cannot be supervised in this way, you have the wrong people on your team.

The whole point of intentional living with Key Result Areas, Annual Ministry Plans, and personal retreat days is to unleash people while maintaining maximum alignment and accountability. These tools provide a road map to follow that, with the agreement of supervisors, gives people the skills to manage themselves.

This understanding changes the equation for every supervisor. With the right people living and working intentionally in their sweet spots, you no longer need to manage. Your job changes to coaching and mentoring. Which would you prefer? Your people know which they prefer.

As we talk about mentoring and coaching in this chapter, I am going to make a distinction between the two. They are different sides of the same coin, each with its own focuses. A good team leader needs to practice both, depending on the circumstance.

THE PRACTICES OF COACHES

One of my great privileges is to coach a number of people. Having passed the fifty-year mark, my real work now is to unleash the next generation of leaders in our organization and in the church. So I make a personal commitment to coach, formally or informally, ten people at any time. Some of these are people who report to me; others are simply those in whom I see great potential.

Coaches release people's gifting and potential. Coaching is not about helping others become like us! Or having them do things the way we would. The world does not need another one of "us." Coaches release the gifting and potential in others and help them become as successful as they can possibly be.

Release is a key word for a coach. God has gifted people with unique skills and particular ways of approaching problems and situations. Coaches want to tap this potential and pull out these gifts so they are released in increasingly productive and effective ways.

Leaders who think life is all about them will never make good coaches (nor do they deserve to have good people working for them). Coaching is one of the most selfless activities we can do because coaches focus on helping others be successful and allowing them to get the credit. The most loved and effective leaders are those who take this approach toward those they lead. When our people know we are committed to making them successful, they become the most loyal team members we have.

This is consistent with what we have already noted: Leaders must lead through their teams. The more successful team members are, the more effective the leader is.

Coaches don't tell; they ask. Releasing others' potential means our challenge is not to tell people how we would do things but to coach them to solve problems and meet challenges themselves. Coaches ask questions—lots of questions, questions that make others think and come to good conclusions. This is a challenge for many leaders who are ready to tell others what to do (and that's necessary on occasion). Releasing people, however, means helping *them* decide how to proceed.

One of my most trusted colleagues, Gary, is the best I have ever seen at asking questions. Sometimes I have to say, "Enough already!" He probes, questions, circles back to ask a different way—always trying to clarify and help you think. Through his questions he helps people understand motives, gifting, options, potential solutions, and ways to achieve maximum impact.

Because coaching is interactive, we need to take time to dialogue. For people who live on the fly this means a change of approach. On-the-fly people have no option but to tell others what to do; they don't have time for anything else. But this method disempowers others. Caring about others and their development means we are willing and committed to take time with them, whether face-to-face, by phone, or (as often happens in our global organization) by using communications software.

Coaches care about the whole person. Many leaders and organizations simply use people. Such organizations don't make the annual "best places to work" list. While good organizations, teams, and leaders are deeply missional, coaches understand there are many factors in people's lives that affect their work and emotional health. Caring about the whole person is one of the keys to unlocking potential.

A constellation of issues should be explored on a monthly basis with those you lead. I frequently ask people in our organization, "What is your happiness factor?" (on a scale of one to ten). I am not specifying only job-related answers. I want to know how the individual is doing generally. If I get less than a seven, I follow up with, "What is going on?" Most often, people are frank in their responses. If the answer is job-related, whether or not I can do anything about it, at least I know there is an issue. If it is a personal issue, I can at least pray. And the individuals know I care—about them (not just their work).

If the issue is job-related, I often ask, "What would make your happiness factor greater?" Sometimes I find out that someone is feeling boxed in, a supervisor is not empowering, or an employee is bored and needs a greater challenge. The question allows me to see if we can solve the issue. But again, people know I care—and when I follow up they *really* know I care.

Coaches are exegetes of those they coach. People cannot be treated in a cookie-cutter manner. Individuals are just that — individuals — and our approaches need to fit who they are and how they are wired.

I have had great people on a variety of teams. One of them would periodically come into my office and need to talk — maybe for forty-five minutes or so. He wanted me to know what was happening in his area. Sometimes he sought counsel, but it was really "connection" time. Once done, he worked in a highly productive manner, but the connection time was crucial.

Another team member likes to pop in two to three times a week. She sits down, debriefs, and then pops out again. She will give me crucial information she thinks I need to hear and then leave it with me.

My assistant needs context for issues. If she fully understands the context, she is highly productive. When I ask her to work with me on a project, I know that giving her the context will help her do what she needs to do.

Our organization does a fair amount of testing to help people understand their wiring. That testing also helps supervisors know how to work with, coach, and mentor employees in ways consistent with their wiring. I want my team members to understand my wiring as well. The better we understand one another, the better we work together, find synergies, avoid conflict, and encourage each other.

Coaches hold people with an open hand. The ultimate test of whether we want the best for those who work with us is whether we hold them with an open hand. Are we willing to develop them for their sakes even if it means we end up developing them out of the organization?

Wanting the best for people engenders huge loyalty and appreciation. Holding people with an open hand communicates that, ultimately, we care about them and what God wants for their lives, not what we want or can get out of them.

People belong to God, not us. Our commitment ought to be to help them be the most effective they can be, become everything they can become, and use their gifts to the maximum. If this is our commitment, people will know and appreciate our care. If it is not our commitment, people will know and resent our attempt to control.

I tell those who report to me on my senior team that I will always seek the best for them, will help them develop and thrive, and will never stand in their way should God lead them elsewhere (even though it would not be my choice). I also ask them to trust me and tell me if they are thinking of leaving so we can at least talk. If I can change something that would keep them engaged with us, I want the opportunity to do so. If they are clearly being led elsewhere, I want to help them in the transition. Of course I cannot mandate this, but because team members believe I want the best for them, it has happened in almost every instance.

Coaches always try to keep their people engaged. People, especially highly motivated people, are not static. They grow, they change, they get bored, and they need new challenges. My philosophy is that I want to find the very best people I can find and then keep them highly motivated by changing their responsibilities when I need to.

One is better off being flexible with job responsibilities and therefore keeping great people than seeing them go because the organization is not flexible enough. At each annual review I ask, "If there were things you could change about your job, what would they be?" With good people, I do my best to reconfigure to keep them as engaged as possible.

THE PRACTICES OF MENTORS

If being a coach is one side of the coin, being a mentor is the other. Mentors are more direct than coaches, in order to help those they lead grow and move to the next level of effectiveness. Taken together, the practices of mentors and coaches give a healthy balance to the supervisory role.

Mentors give honest feedback. Constructive feedback is often missing in ministry organizations, where the culture is supposed to be "nice." The lack of honest feedback hurts both the individual and the organization. It does no one any favors and can result in people being let go for behaviors that might have been modified if someone had been courageous enough to be honest.

Kay, a missionary in Europe (name and location have been changed), has a strong personality. She comes across as demanding (what she needs from her people, she needs now) and arrogant (she does not listen to what others have to say). Kay has a history of short tenure in any one place since no team is good enough for her and, consequently, no one wants to work with her.

The only way to help her is for a supervisor to be absolutely honest about how her behaviors affect other people (both missionaries and nationals) and the fact that her behaviors are not acceptable in an organization that places a high priority on healthy people and healthy teams. A healthy mentor will give honest feedback and clarify which behaviors are acceptable within the organization and which are not. And then hold her accountable!

Mentors get people necessary intervention. Kay and others like her need some intense time with a professional trained to help people understand their behaviors and their negative impact on others. Good mentors not only provide honest feedback but also, where necessary, insist employees or team members receive help that will allow them to be more effective.

In our organization, this often means help from a psychologist or a good mentor, especially regarding behaviors that negatively affect the employee and the people around him or her. Our commitment to healthy missionaries and healthy teams makes intervention a necessity when there is significant lack of health. We do it for the sake of the employees, the organization, the team they serve on, and their long-term effectiveness.

Too often, Christian organizations are not redemptive where they need to be, ignoring issues that should be dealt with and compounding the problem by eventually letting people go without ever being honest or getting them needed help. This does not honor the employees, the organization, or God.

Mentors care about their people and a winning team. Leaders build teams that can win. Yes, we know ministry is not about the game. In fact, it is about something far more important: God's kingdom. High-impact leaders are committed to results, insist team members play well together, ensure players are playing to their strengths, and produce results consistent with the mission of the organization.

This means leaders will reorganize teams for effective ministry when necessary. Sometimes this will be done by changing the responsibilities of team members. At other times, leaders need to let people go. Perhaps the time comes when the organization has outgrown a person's capacity. At other times, an individual is not in his or her sweet spot and should no longer be in your organization. Sometimes people are just lazy and unwilling to take the steps to be as productive as you require. Sometimes there is an EQ problem that even mentoring and intervention cannot overcome (or the individual is unwilling to overcome).

Once you conclude the situation is not going to change and *you* need to make a change, do it as quickly as possible, with the best counsel you can get. You want to be legally compliant from an HR perspective—and be smart, since team members have constituencies. Be as generous as you need to be so that when people inquire, you can justify both the decision you made and the process you followed. But don't ignore the problem. It will only create greater issues if not dealt with wisely and quickly.

We want to be grace filled and redemptive, but good leaders do not allow the mission to be compromised by keeping ineffective people.

THE MENTOR/COACH MONTHLY MEETING

High-impact mentor/coaches avoid two traps ministry people often fall into. The first is to assume everything is fine and not spend one-on-one time with direct reports because it is a distraction. The second is to micromanage reports and disempower them by not allowing them to develop their areas of ministry. Neither practice will help you develop a results-oriented, aligned, and productive team.

A best practice is to schedule a monthly meeting where you can play both the mentor and the coach, encouraging, providing feedback, removing barriers, and ensuring people are tracking with their Key Result Areas and Annual Ministry Plans.

Your monthly meetings should take place after people's monthly personal retreat days. During their days, they should fill out a monthly report form, which becomes the basis for your meeting. Our organization uses the following form.

MONTHLY STAFF FEEDBACK

Please complete as part of your personal retreat day and forward to your supervisor.

1. On a scale of one to ten, my "happiness factor" this month is _____.
(1 = Low and 10 = High)

2. I need a decision or information from you on the following items:

3. Relationship(s) with the following person/people have "gone sideways" recently:

4. I'm having a problem with the following roadblock(s):

5. Here are the results of my top three priorities from last month:

6. Here are my top three ministry/work priorities for next month:

7. Currently, my most challenging issue is:

8. Here's how I am doing in the following areas:
(0 = Awful, 2 = Not well, 4 = Slipping, 6 = OK, 8 = Very good, 10 = Great)

_____Spiritually   _____ Mentally   _____Emotionally
_____Physically   _____Relationally   _____Personal Evangelism

Further comments I would like to share with you about these areas:

9. You can be praying for me and/or my team regarding the following:

This short form gives the mentor/coach valuable information about his or her people. Whether the answers are covered in the monthly meeting depends on what is recorded. A good mentor/coach wants to understand the issues people are struggling with, what they need from their supervisor, what they are working on, and the results of their past month's priorities. These questions are designed to help supervisors understand where their people are in the following areas.

1. "My 'happiness factor' this month." As explained earlier, the point of this question is to find out where people are generally. Their answers will be a combination of various factors: some professional, some personal, some related to circumstances. Whatever the number is, the follow-up question is, "Why? What is contributing to the number?" Questions such as, "What would make it higher?" or "What are the contributing factors to your number this month?" can help you scope out areas of concern, joy, frustration, or motivation that are influencing your team member.

By asking this question monthly, you "take the temperature" of team members and uncover information that can help you understand and coach them more effectively. You also have an early warning system that can help you keep individuals motivated and fulfilled in their jobs rather than finding out one day, to your consternation, that they are unhappy and moving on.

2. "I need a decision or information from you." This question informs or reminds the supervisor that something is needed before team members can move forward.

3. "Relationship(s) with the following person/people have 'gone sideways.'" Relationships that are not in sync are a common dysfunction; left alone, they harm cooperation, trust, effectiveness, and integration. This question helps your reports keep short accounts and quickly deal with relational breakdowns. As a mentor/coach, you have the opportunity to help team members determine how best to repair broken relationships or deal with conflicts. It also sends a powerful message to team members that your organization (and you as their leader) is committed to healthy relationships and the principles of Matthew 18.

4. "I'm having a problem with the following roadblock(s)." Roadblocks are issues that need to be resolved before your team members can move forward, but which they cannot resolve by themselves. They may need the cooperation of another individual or department. It could be a funding issue, a decision, or an organizational barrier that someone at a higher level needs to resolve.

A key responsibility of leaders is to remove barriers for those who report to them. Where there are barriers, commit to a plan showing how you will help remove the barrier, put it on your calendar, and carry through as promised.

5. and 6. "The results of my top three priorities from last month" and "My top three ministry/work priorities for next month." These two questions go to the heart of intentionality. If people cannot identify their top priorities for the coming month, they are not carefully planning during their personal retreat days. These three priorities must tie back to their KRAs and AMPs. If the supervisor does not believe the priorities listed are truly strategic, this gives an opportunity to dialogue.

Equally important is requiring an update on the results of last month's priorities. Remember, leaders care about results. Asking the question, probing where necessary, and holding direct reports accountable sends a strong message that results matter. When there is a pattern of unacceptable or unfulfilled results, the leader has concrete and objective means to discuss the issue of performance.

This is also where you can ask how your reports are doing in their Annual Ministry Plans—a monthly reminder that you expect the plan is being worked on and will, in large part, be fulfilled. Neither you nor they should be surprised at the end of the year regarding the AMPs because you have been discussing them monthly.

7. "My most challenging issue." The issue may be one you know about; often it will not be since you are not aware of all that goes on in your reports' world. Since it is a challenge to them, it gives you an opportunity to mentor/coach. Ask questions, probe, and help them discover ways they might approach the challenge. Challenges are growth points when handled well, so you will want to pay close attention to these areas and how your reports are handling them.

8. "How I am doing in the areas of my life." The essence of the mentor/coach relationship is caring about the whole person. Even asking the question means your reports must think about these important life areas monthly and determine a grade. It is a reminder that health in all aspects of life matters—and influences their lives at work. It also tells them you care about them as a person, not simply for what you can get out of them as an employer. Low scores and good questions about any area can spark a healthy conversation about what they are doing or could do to bring their scores up.

9. "You can be praying for me and/or my team regarding the following." As a leader, you model dependence on God by taking the time on a regular basis to pray for those special requests and then follow up with the staff member.

MAXIMIZING THE MONTHLY COACH/MENTOR MEETING

A commitment high-impact leaders make to those they lead is that they will set aside quality time to meet with them monthly. In the best-case scenario, this meeting is face-to-face, but in global organizations it will often be by phone or using technology like Skype or NetMeeting. The key is for supervisors to engage fully—mentally and emotionally—during this time, giving the best they have to those they supervise.

Though you have asked your team members to bring a structured report to the meeting, I suggest you do not rigidly follow an outline for the meeting but vary it so discussions do not degenerate into boring or routine dialogues.

Start by getting a feel for what is happening in your team members' lives. The small talk matters because it reinforces relationship and because we're affected by the stuff of life, good and bad. You also want to know your team members as well as you can, so even small details matter.

While you may talk through specific issues surfaced by the report, you should also ask some well-thought-out questions that will allow you to probe in areas where your team members need growth. I make a list before the meeting of issues and questions I want to talk about so my contribution as a mentor/coach is as productive as it can be. I also think through the approach I will take in areas where my team members might react defensively. I want to get at issues without raising unnecessary walls. I am there to help, not hurt them. Wherever possible I will use questions to get at issues I want to address.

When direct feedback is required, I will say something such as, "Let me give you feedback on how you reacted in our meeting," or "I'm going to coach you on this issue." In the case of significant performance issues, it pays to be direct and provide clearly defined expectations for performance improvements.

When there are performance issues, always make a written record of your conversation and send a copy to your team member of the issues you discussed and the action steps you require. Not only are you making your evaluation and expectations clear, but you are also keeping a paper trail in the event you need to let the person go. You want a clear record of the process you used to rectify the situation before termination. Keep those records in a secure place in case legal action is threatened or taken against the organization.

As you walk through the monthly mentor/coach meeting, keep notes on key issues so you can review them prior to your next meeting. In addition, keep an electronic or hard copy of the monthly report form for future review.

H. I. BEST PRACTICE

The strategy with problematic people is to keep shrinking their boxes and clarifying your expectations until their performance improves, they decide to leave because of the pain, or you have the evidence you need to let them go.

With good team members, keep expanding the box of empowerment. People who perform well deserve expanded freedom.

MENTORING/COACHING THROUGH ANNUAL PERFORMANCE REVIEWS

In the absence of KRAs and AMPs, annual reviews are a frustrating experience for supervisors and team members. The frustration comes in quantifying success, identifying clear expectations, and sorting out results from activity. The discussion can be a nebulous evaluation around foggy expectations—even with great team members.

KRAs and AMPs change the whole equation. There is now an objective basis on which team members can evaluate their own performances (our goal is to help people lead themselves) and on which supervisors can evaluate them.

Because of the monthly mentor/coach meeting, there should never be a surprise during an annual evaluation. If there are surprises, it means the supervisor has not been giving honest feedback along the way. Frankly, that is unfair to the team members. Team members should have a very good idea what their supervisor will say at the annual evaluation.

Annual reviews are tied directly to KRAs and AMPs. Thus the first step is for the team member to do a self-evaluation. A sample form that can be used as the basis for the review follows.

STAFF MEMBER ANNUAL REVIEW

Name:_____Date:_____

1. Comments on KRA accomplishments:

2. What is mission critical for this next year and needs to be reflected in next year's KRAs and AMPs?

3. Comments about relational growth this past year:

4. Comments about personal growth this past year:

5. What personal development goals need to be included in next year's KRAs and AMPs?

6. Comments about general work/ministry effectiveness:

7. Recommendations for any necessary growth/ development:

Supervisor's signature: _____

Staff member's signature: _____

During the meeting, team leaders sit down with their direct reports to discuss the areas identified by the form.

1. "Comments on KRA accomplishments." This evaluation is a straightforward process. During the year we want team members to have "worked the plan." The percentage of their plans they have worked is a key indicator of their success for the year. All one needs to do at annual reviews is consider the AMPs under each KRA and comment on what team members have accomplished during the year.

A perfect score is not necessarily the goal. When people first start to use KRAs and AMPs they are often optimistic as to how much they can accomplish in one year. In addition, life happens; sometimes it is simply not possible to complete the plans. What you want to see are intentionality and a high degree of follow-through. Those two combined will likely help people accomplish far more than they were previously able to.

2. "What is mission critical for this next year and needs to be reflected in next year's KRAs and AMPs?" Generally, KRAs do not change unless responsibilities have changed. Before you meet for the review, your reports should have completed an annual planning retreat, filled out their part of the evaluations, and completed their AMPs for the coming year.

Your best people will always be harder on themselves than you will be. Celebrate with them the wins they have experienced in the past year and be clear on how their work has positively contributed to the organization and its mission. Thank them for the part they have played on your team!

The annual review then provides an opportunity to look forward and dialogue about the KRAs and AMPs they identified for the coming year. Those KRAs and AMPs should logically continue to drive their ministry down the road and build on what has already been accomplished. There should be a direct connection between one year's plans and the next.

3. "Comments about relational growth." Competent people continue to grow relationally throughout their lifetimes. Given the importance of EQ, leaders should dialogue with reports about areas where growth would be helpful.

4. and 5. "Comments about personal growth" and **"What personal development goals need to be included in next year's KRAs and AMPs?"** The personal-growth KRA is always listed first because it affects spiritual, emotional, professional, and family lives. For believers, it is core to who we are and who we want to become. For this reason, dialogue on these questions is significant in an annual review. When people get into trouble, it is almost inevitable that an area of their personal lives has been neglected.

Supervisors owe it to their reports to probe, encourage, ask good questions, and help them be all they can be in this area of life.

This should naturally lead into the question of what needs to be honed in personal growth in the coming year and whether the AMPs reflect the necessary priorities. Make specific suggestions where you think development would strategically enhance team members' work.

6. "Comments about general work/ministry effectiveness." Because our focus is not on activity but on results, this question goes to the heart of how team members and supervisors see overall effectiveness. Are team members playing at the level needed in their jobs and on your team? Are they using their time and energies in the most strategic ways and concentrating on true priorities? Are they finding ways to leverage their work for greater effectiveness? Are they doing multiplication rather than addition? Is their work focused on missional rather than ancillary issues?

One question a supervisor should ask in the midst of this discussion is, "What do you need to do next year to go to the next level of effectiveness in your ministry?" Every year, each of us ought to be able to identify several areas where we can take the next step by delegating something, reprioritizing our time, or making a few strategic decisions. Helping reports identify these steps for the next year will help them grow in their ministry. These should then be reflected in their AMPs.

7. "Recommendations for any necessary growth/development." Because mentor/coaches want the best for their people, they will give careful thought to additional growth and development opportunities that have not already been covered. We want each team member to grow in significant ways every year.

H. I. BEST PRACTICE

Tie annual evaluations to the close of one ministry year and the start of another, not team members' anniversary dates. This way, annual reviews are tied directly to the completion of KRAs and AMPs and the start of a new round of both.

THE SELF-LEADERSHIP OF MENTOR/COACHES

High-impact leaders can mentor/coach only if the way they live their own lives gives their mentoring, coaching, and leadership intrinsic authority. People will follow those who garner respect, who live what they talk, and who are out in front of those they lead. Without the moral authority that comes from self-leadership, they will engender only cynicism.

Self-leadership requires us to set the pace through personal development and growth; a high degree of intentionality and discipline; living the rhythm of KRAs, AMPs, and personal retreat days; and a commitment to results that is based on well thought through priorities. Those we lead know whether we live that way or not. In fact, as good as the suggestions in this book may be, if you are not willing to walk the walk, don't ask your team members to do it. We must lead the way in ongoing professional, personal, emotional, spiritual, and missional growth — or move aside and let someone else lead.

The issues in this chapter apply to leaders first and foremost. Lived out, they become part of our lives and then naturally overflow into those we lead. As Jesus said, we are the overflow of our hearts. We can fake it for a season, but not for long. I have made my KRAs and AMPs public to the organization I lead. They have a right to know that I live by the disciplines I ask of them. Are you willing to do the same?

H. I. BEST PRACTICE

A best practice for leaders is to ask their direct reports to contribute to their own annual evaluation in a 360-degree feedback process. We may think we are modeling what we espouse, but what do those who work for us think? How about asking them? There is nothing like honest input from teams to help leaders know how they are doing and where they can grow. This requires an attitude of "nothing to prove and nothing to lose" and a real desire on the part of the team leader to accept constructive feedback and continue to grow in his or her leadership.

WHO ARE YOUR MENTOR/COACHES?

The higher the position a person holds in a ministry organization, the less likely he or she is to be coached and mentored by someone else in the organization. Who coaches you? Who holds you accountable for intentionality and results? Hopefully you have a board that does some of that, but boards may or may not know what you are doing (it is more likely for a board to be involved in this level of coaching in a local church where boards meet more often).

H. I. MOMENT

List the mentors in your life:

_____

_____

_____

I can count about ten mentors in my life. They include the senior team I serve on, my coleader in the organization I lead, a brother, my father, two close friends, and a handful of others. In addition, I intentionally cultivate friendships with people I believe I can learn from and contribute to. Almost everything I practice I have learned from others. The moment I think I am self-sufficient is when it is over for me as a leader.

If I were to slip from the life I espouse, there are people around me who would gently but honestly confront me. Who are those people for you?

High-impact leaders make themselves accountable by bringing around them other leaders who consistently ask good questions, even when the questions are uncomfortable. They develop a constellation of mentors/coaches (no one mentor can meet all of our needs) whom they meet with to learn from and grow. They read to learn from others. And they discipline their own lives so they can lead by example first and teaching second.

H. I. QUESTIONS

For Team Leaders

How does the mentor/coach paradigm described in this chapter compare to your approach? What changes do you need to make?

What style of management do you personally prefer? Why?

How good are you at providing honest feedback to your reports?

Who are your mentors? What do they provide for you?

For Team Discussion

What style of management do you prefer? Why?

Which mentor/coach practices described in this chapter would help you do a better job in your role?

Who are your mentors, besides your supervisor? What do they provide for you?

CHAPTER NINE

DANGEROUS TRANSITIONS

CHAPTER SUMMARY:

Organizational leadership transitions are dangerous moments, regardless of the level at which they take place.

Transitions must be handled with great care if they are to succeed. This includes understanding the leadership pipeline within the organization — the various levels of leadership and the specific sets of competencies and values that must characterize each level.

Not everyone is wired to be a leader. To place people in leadership who are not wired to lead is to hurt them and those they lead. Remember, too, that everyone has a capacity beyond which he or she will not be successful. Thus, the process of leadership selection is critical.

In order for these transitions to succeed, it is crucial that transitioning leaders are closely mentored and actively coached throughout the process. Part of this transition is helping them give up the values and requirements of the prior level and take on the values and requirements of the new level.

Most organizations do a substandard job of identifying and training a leadership "bench." Some organizations are not even friendly to leaders. Good leaders are always identifying potential leaders and have a process in place to groom them for the next leadership level.

Negotiating transitional moments for success is a high priority of good leaders and healthy organizations.

Why do some people who transition from one level of leadership to another succeed while others fail?

Many leadership transitions are painful—both for the leader and for those being led. Few moments are more dangerous for leaders and organizations than these transitions. If they fail, they hurt people on the team and damage the confidence and ability of the one who is making the transition.

A TRUE STORY

Dave was a successful recruiter for a ministry organization. Year after year he excelled at recruiting personnel for short-term teams; he also led a team of other recruiters, most of them just out of college. Dave's team liked him; he could communicate well, was mission driven, and had a good reputation in his organization.

Because of his skills, Dave caught the attention of a Christian placement organization. When a senior position in a denominational office came along, he was convinced to put his name in the hat. The denomination was looking for someone who would serve at a senior-team level and lead a team of highly qualified professionals in several divisions. They interviewed a number of candidates with long lists of credentials, without success. They didn't fit the culture of the denomination, they led in ways inconsistent with the denomination's leadership model, or they simply were not qualified.

When Dave's resume came in, it looked impressive. Several interviews went exceedingly well. Dave had done his homework and knew what to ask. He was confident and articulate, and all his references strongly supported him for the position. The denomination hired Dave with great anticipation of his success.

Quickly, however, warning signs appeared. Dave spent a great deal of time in his office with his door closed, leaving staff members wondering what he was up to. He listened very little when he met with staff members and didn't ask questions about their areas of responsibility. In senior staff meetings, he often seemed to be in his own world and was not engaged in issues the team was dealing with. He skipped and cancelled meetings with the team he led. Furthermore, his supervisor found there were serious gaps between his understanding of Dave's responsibilities and how Dave saw his job.

Dave's team was patient with their new leader, but one by one they expressed doubts to their prior supervisor about Dave's fitness for the leadership role. What had been a cohesive team started to fragment as members began doing their own thing. Their previous camaraderie was gone. Dave's supervisor continued to spend time with him and assumed the pain was simply a result of a leadership transition.

He was wrong. After a year of substandard results, Dave's supervisor started to confront the issues more directly. As the supervisor started more intentional coaching, Dave withdrew into his world more and more. Eighteen months after his hire, Dave resigned and went back to recruiting.

What went wrong here? The denomination had used a qualified search firm, procedural due diligence had been followed, references had been checked, coaching and appropriate supervision had taken place, and Dave was a person of character with a history of success. Yet in spite of his confidence and skills, he had not been able to fulfill his job responsibilities. Dave's success as a team leader had been strong in his previous position, but in this one it was not. The leadership transition did not work, and Dave, his team, his supervisor, and the organization paid the price. All felt like they had somehow failed in the process.

THE RAMIFICATIONS OF TRANSITION

Leadership transitions are dangerous moments at whatever level they take place. When they go well, everyone is happy. When they go wrong, the organization suffers. Sometimes good people choose to leave because they feel they were dealt a bad deck when they were given a dysfunctional or unqualified leader.

In analyzing this transition, the supervisor looked at the level Dave had played at in his prior organization and realized he had led a midlevel team of young people. At the denominational office, he was leading a senior-level team of proven professionals. In addition, while Dave saw himself as a great team leader, he understood "team" as a group of people who spent a lot of time together with lots of social interaction. The team at the new job centered on mission, not fellowship, and Dave did not know how to lead a missional team. He was also intimidated by the professionalism of those he led.

Dave had been promoted above his current level of competency and was positioned to fail. His failure was not a reflection of his character or his basic competency. He had missed some key leadership transitions on the way to leading at that higher level.

Transitional moments must be handled with great care if they are to succeed. The stakes are high because if the transition fails, the implications affect everyone who works for the new or promoted leader. Issues like EQ, job fit, understanding of the role, knowing how to lead and coach others, servant leadership, communication skills, ability to gain the respect of those being led, organizational understanding, and proper leadership maturity for the new role are all crucial. Given the complexity, it is no wonder so many transitions run into trouble.

One of my colleagues, Daryl Anderson, did an extensive study of leadership transitions within our organization by asking two important questions. Notice the top ten answers he received to each one:

Question 1: "When you have observed someone who did not transition well from one leadership position to the next, what were the reasons?"

Top Responses:
1. Lack of adequate preparation, training, and orientation to the new position
2. Wrong assumptions and expectations about fit and needs for new ministry
3. Could not switch from doing ministry to leading others to do ministry

4. Lack of EQ/people skills
5. Lack of gifting for the position
6. Could not switch out of former role into a new role with a new set of needed competencies and priorities
7. Did not understand the organizational changes from one level to the next
8. Was not able to manage a larger ministry
9. Could not switch between self-motivation and instruction to motivating and instructing others
10. Promoted because of longevity in the mission rather than gifting for the new position

Question 2: "When you have observed people who *did* transition well from one level of leadership to the next, what were the reasons the transition went well?"

Top Responses:
1. Active coaching throughout the transition
2. Good preparation for the transition
3. Strong sense of call that was affirmed by others
4. Adequate knowledge of the ministry they would be leading
5. Good communication skills
6. Displayed real concern for the people they were leading
7. Possessed healthy EQ
8. Clear that they were gifted for the role — in their sweet spots
9. Exhibited a servant heart — leadership was not about them but others
10. Learned the job well and approached it with a learning spirit

Our organization was forced to look carefully at how we made these transitions. Historically we had not highly valued leadership positions, had not proactively trained people before they were placed into leadership roles, and had fostered an administrative role for leaders rather than a strong leadership role. Often people were placed with no evaluation of leadership ability. Sometimes people moved into leadership roles because they were the only ones willing, because they had shown success at something else, or because they were popular with their peers.

The results were mixed. Where leadership ability was low, those reporting to the new leaders felt significant frustration. Where it was high, the success was more about God's mercy than good planning. One of the first issues I was confronted with as the senior leader was that we had nonleaders in leadership roles who were causing angst, frustration, and conflict. My consulting experience tells me we are not the only organization that has paid too little attention to whom we put into leadership roles and how we train people for those roles. In this regard, ministries are far behind the secular world.

One of the unhealthy cultural realities of ministry organizations (this is especially true of mission organizations, but it infects others as well) is that personnel see themselves as "independent contractors" who have been hired to do their own thing. Denominations see this mentality when various levels do not work with each other. Churches see this in siloed ministries that pay no attention to the rest of the church's ministry. Mission organizations see this when missionaries view their sending organization as simply a nice way of getting to the field, but perceive no corresponding responsibility back to it.

The thesis of this book, of course, is that this kind of thinking will never make for high-impact teams or ministry. Issues of leadership, alignment, missional focus, intentional plans, and integrated efforts are all critical to making the greatest ministry impact. The people we place into leadership and how we prepare them for their roles become important pieces in this puzzle. One of the first places we start is by identifying the leadership pipelines within our organizations.

UNDERSTANDING LEADERSHIP PIPELINES

A great deal of study has been done about what is called the leadership pipeline.[1] The thesis is that every organization has levels of leadership that need to be taken into account when making leadership transitions.

For instance, in our mission organization there are six distinct levels of leadership:

1. *Self-leader.* This applies to all personnel (intentional living for personal and ministry development).
2. *Ministry leader.* Leads a particular ministry on a team.
3. *Team leader.* Spends 50 percent of time leading others on his or her team. Has completed team-leader training.
4. *Area leader.* Full-time leader who leads other ministry-team leaders and is responsible for the management of multiple teams. Reports to an international leader and has completed area-leadership training.
5. *International leader.* Reports to executive director; has broad area of ReachGlobal (RG) responsibility, including leader, ministry, and organizational development; leads one of the five RG divisions.
6. *EFCA senior vice president.* Responsible for all RG ministries, leads RG senior team, serves on the EFCA senior team, and answers to the EFCA president.

The rule of the leadership pipeline is that one should never promote someone from one level to a higher one without insisting they move through each level in between. Why? Because every level of leadership requires a specific set of competencies. Moving from one level of leadership to the next is always a transition.

When Joel, discussed in an earlier chapter, had difficulty flying at 30,000 feet and wanted to dip down to 5,000 feet to do things he had previously done, the issue was trouble transitioning from one level to another. If we allow people to skip a level of leadership, they are missing the critical information and experience they need to do further levels well.

That was also the struggle of Dave the recruiter. He had missed at least two stages in the pipeline, leaving him without the core competencies to lead a team at the higher level. Neither Dave, the search firm, nor the denomination recognized he was not ready for the level of leadership he was being hired for. He was destined to struggle and ultimately fail in the new position.

It is not important that potential leaders have navigated all levels of the pipeline in *your* organization. It is not unusual for us to bring some-one into ReachGlobal from the marketplace. What we want to know is that they have gone through similar levels and not skipped any crucial stages.

Identify your pipeline. Unless your organization understands the differing roles at each bend in the leadership pipeline, you run signifi-cant risk of a difficult or failed transition. The role of an independent producer (someone who basically works independently and does hands-on work) is very different from that of a team leader who must lead through others. And that role is very different from someone who super-vises multiple team leaders. Each level brings different competencies, job descriptions, scopes of vision, and ways of thinking about life.

To illustrate, I will use the example of leadership levels among the staff members of a large church.

1. *Support-staff member.* Primarily provides administrative support without a lot of decision making. The focus is primarily on one's own work. The typical ministry volunteer also fits in this slot. Flies at 5,000 feet.
2. *Support-staff leader.* Provides administrative support and gives leadership to other staff members. Required to mentor and coach others; build a strong, unified, results-oriented team; organize effectively for the best results; and manage conflict. The focus is on managing one's own work and ensuring that the team is doing well and that direct reports are managing their work well. Volunteer ministry-team leaders fit here as well. Flies at 10,000 feet.
3. *Pastor/administrator.* Leads a particular ministry or support area. Required to be a self-starter, self-manage through KRAs and AMPs, use time efficiently, work with others in a staff

team, possess high EQ, and communicate and work well with others. Responsible for own area of work and probably deploys and leads a team of volunteers. Focus is missional, primarily on own area but also aligned with other ministries. Span of control and responsibility is significant but focused on own ministry. Flies at 15,000 feet.

4. *Supervisor of pastors or administrators.* Leads a team of professionals focused on a specific area of ministry (such as youth or children). Required to be a self-starter, self-manage through KRAs and AMPs, empower others, use time efficiently, lead through others, possess high EQ, and communicate and work well with others. Must build a strong, unified, aligned, results-oriented team; be responsible for results of the team's work; and mentor/coach team members. Focus is missional, primarily on others to ensure the success of the team. Span of control and responsibility is significantly larger than in previous level, requiring the ability to think more globally. Flies at 20,000 feet.

5. *Executive pastor.* Same as previous level with the additional requirement to take into account the whole ministry of the church, be an excellent team builder, and keep everyone focused on the mission, values, central ministry focus, and ethos of the church, with a focus on results. In addition, must be able to negotiate multiple constituencies, including the staff, board, and senior pastor. Fingerprints are on everything, but name is on nothing. Quintessential servant leader who keeps the ministry in alignment and people working together. This requires a high level of EQ, an ability to lead from behind the scenes, and a humble servant-leadership style. Flies at 30,000 feet.

6. *Senior pastor.* Senior leader of the organization with three primary focal points: preaching (either personally or by leading a teaching team); developing the mission and vision of the church and guarding its values and ethos; and developing, empowering, and releasing key leaders. Is the senior mentor/

coach, looks at the ministry horizon, is deeply missional, thinks globally, and assembles the highest quality leadership team. Keeper of the vision and senior motivator for missional results. Must possess a high EQ, have a humble spirit, be personally aware, and be comfortable with self. Flies at 40,000 feet.

H. I. MOMENT

Consider the different responsibilities and competencies required at each level in the sample church pipeline just described. Identify the differences between each of the six levels. Then identify the five or six leadership pipeline levels in your organization.

1. _____

2. _____

3. _____

4. _____

5. _____

6. _____

For each leadership level, determine necessary competencies and skills, and establish training. After you have identified your leadership-pipeline levels, you can determine the competencies needed for each level and the training that is imperative if someone is to succeed there. A rule of thumb is that the higher the level in the pipeline, the more training and mentoring/coaching you will want to do.

ReachGlobal has identified a common curriculum required for each level of our pipeline. This gives each leadership level shared vocabulary, training, and skill development across our global organization. This also makes it possible to transfer a leader to a position at the same level somewhere else in the world and to train leaders for the next level in the pipeline.

In addition, at the top two senior-leadership levels, all potential leaders must undergo a testing process that measures their capacities, leadership styles, wiring, supervisory styles, and passions to ensure they are a good fit for the job. Often, such testing confirms what we already think. Sometimes, the testing indicates the leader is wired to fly at a lower altitude (they will do better with more hands-on work). We will never knowingly place someone in a leadership position we don't believe he or she is capable of fulfilling.

Be willing to say no to potential leaders who are not qualified or not ready. One of the hardest things to do is to be discerning about people we love and respect and to honor their wiring and qualifications when we're considering them for leadership roles. There are three rules that must be honored in this regard.

One: Not everyone is wired to lead. To place people in leadership who are not gifted for leadership is to hurt them and those they lead.

Two: Everyone has a capacity ceiling beyond which he or she will not be successful. We want to grow people to the highest level we can, but once they hit that capacity ceiling, we must honor it or we dishonor them and those they lead. A capacity limit may come from the necessity to think globally, the altitude required, the span of responsibility, the level of strategy and planning necessary, or the level of mentoring/coaching called for. If you promote people beyond their capacity ceilings, you set them up to fail.

Three: Never make a hiring or promotion decision by yourself. It is simply too dangerous. All of us have blind spots, or we can be enamored by how people interview and present themselves. If leaders in our organization are going to promote someone, they must secure permission from the next two levels of leadership. We take leadership seriously and want to ensure that due diligence has been done, that the leadership pipeline has not been violated, and that the transitioning leader is totally in sync with the mission, guiding principles, central ministry focus, and culture of the organization. If there are any red flags, the person doesn't get promoted at that time.

As indicated earlier, we also take testing seriously, particularly at the top two critical levels of leadership. If our testing does not verify our thinking, we will not move forward. We use the services of a job-placement professional who conducts the testing and helps us interpret the results. He does not tell us what we ought to do, but we want to know his opinion on the fit between the job and the potential leader.

These three rules help us resist the temptation to do the easy thing in cases where we really need a leader (never settle for less than you need), or the nice thing in cases where we really want to please someone who wants the job and whom we like. Both temptations are real. Both are dangerous.

Ensure transitioning leaders are actively coached and mentored. Leadership transitions are rarely easy, even for good leaders. We should not expect these changes to be uneventful since people are moving to the next level of leadership—territory in which they have not previously operated. In most cases, they will have made past transitions, so they at least know a major change is coming. In these transitions, it is critical that your transitioning leaders understand the following:

- How the new job differs from the old job
- What they must give up
- What they must do that is new
- How their focus needs to change
- That they will find the transition difficult because there are things they used to do that they really *liked* doing and shouldn't do anymore
- What the organization's expectations are at the new level of leadership
- What reading or training will be required of them
- How you will mentor and coach them in the process
- That you will do 360-degree reviews so you know how those they lead perceive them
- That you will help them grow in their new role

If there is any time for intense mentoring and coaching, this is it. If the transition goes badly, you have lost significant ground and may well lose a good leader and the team members they led. If it is a positive experience, your leadership system gains credibility and your ministry grows.

LEADERS ALWAYS LOOK FOR LEADERS TO DEVELOP

The higher the level of leadership in your pipeline, the harder it is to find competent and qualified leaders. There are two reasons for this. First, even good leaders have built-in capacity ceilings; there truly are fewer people capable of high-level leadership. Second, in many of our organizations we do a substandard job of identifying and training a leadership bench—something that industries and businesses spend a great deal of time, money, and energy doing.

Be on the lookout for leaders at every level of your organization. When you find them, start dialoguing with them about how they are wired and what their passions are. I have found that many in ministry organizations who are wired to lead have not been challenged and are bored in their current roles. Be willing to do some testing to see if the leadership wiring is there.

You will find it easier to identify and develop future leaders if your organization is leader friendly. Many organizations do not empower leaders to lead, but are controlling (this is true of many mission organizations). Good leaders will often self-select out of church or ministry-organization search processes if there is not an empowered culture. They want empowerment and can smell its absence a mile away.

I have noticed in the missions world that a high preponderance of leaders select fields that are "creative access" (not open to traditional missionaries). Why? Because when they look at the traditional fields, they see control, lack of creativity, lack of empowerment, and a controlling ethos. When they look at the creative-access contexts, they say what Chinese warlords out in the hinterlands used to say: "It's a long way to Beijing." Meaning, Beijing (the head office) does not know what they are doing! Organizations that are empowered, healthy, and allow for innovation and creativity will see far more leaders surface than organizations that are not.

H. I. MOMENT

Candidly assess how leader friendly your organization is. If not very friendly, what is needed to change the culture toward its leaders?

When you have surfaced potential leaders, connect them to a mentor/coach (who may or may not be the supervisor) who can help them grow in their leadership abilities. Your organization will only be as good, as healthy, and as effective as your leaders. Good people thrive only under good leadership. Thus, the more you pour into leadership development, the better your organization will be.

This will not happen unless the organization as a whole sees leadership development as a top priority and requires all leaders to be building other leaders. Leadership development will not happen without a built-in, organization-wide system to facilitate it. By making this one of the KRAs of leaders, we ensure that it happens. In addition, by developing training curriculum for each turn in the leadership pipeline, you are requiring every leader to be trained at their level and many for the next level. When you are gone from the scene, your legacy will be the leadership you leave behind.

H. I. QUESTIONS FOR TEAM DISCUSSION

Think through leadership transitions you have been part of or have watched. When they went well, what were the keys to success? When they were rocky, what contributed to the difficulty?

Do you have an intentional coaching plan to ensure that transitioning leaders within your ministry are positioned for success?

What are you and your leadership doing to build a bench of future leaders?

Have you identified the leadership-pipeline levels in your ministry, the competencies needed at each level, and the training required for each level?

POSTSCRIPT

Is building a strong team merely a nice pursuit — or is it a necessary pursuit for long-term missional impact?

That question was answered for me as I was finishing the manuscript of this book.

On December 4, 2007, I woke up almost unable to breathe. My wife, Mary Ann, took me to the emergency room — a visit that turned into an ordeal I should not have survived.

It would be forty-two days in the hospital, thirty-two of them in Intensive Care, battling a highly dreaded and difficult-to-treat MRSA pneumonia — and its attendant complications. I could not go back to work for six weeks after my discharge, and then only part-time. Even as I write this, my energy level is about 60 percent of what it previously was. During this unexpected chapter in my life, the value of a team was reinforced.

Just a few days after I was admitted, the leaders of our personal prayer team flew to town to intercede for me in person. My son Jon informed our larger prayer team and quickly put up a blog that could be accessed only by knowing its address. In the first week, four hundred computers accessed the blog. Over the course of the next month, some eleven thousand unique users had joined the concerted prayer for my life. Blog hits came from seventy-five countries and all fifty states. There is no question in my mind that the concerted prayer of so many and the grace of God were responsible for my healing.

I was out of commission for a full three months and even then was able to work only on a greatly reduced schedule. During that time, absolutely nothing changed in our organization or ministry even though the things I typically did had to be covered by others. The work was able to continue because of the strong teams I work with. The senior team of the EFCA picked up my responsibilities at that level, and the senior team of ReachGlobal picked up my responsibilities there. In fact, they did so well that when I returned I chose not to take back some of my previous responsibilities. I did not need to.

Although I am the senior leader of ReachGlobal, I have chosen to share senior-leadership responsibilities with my wonderful colleague Gary Hunter. Not only does he deeply share the mission, guiding principles, central ministry focus, and health commitments of our sandbox, but he also knows what I know. While we do different things and play to our strengths, the fact that another senior leader was so intimately involved meant he could pick up my responsibilities without the organization missing a heartbeat—and he did.

When team is done well, there is redundancy in the organization. No one person is indispensable. The organization's culture has been so ingrained in the team that even if the leader were to leave, the culture would remain. This will not matter to those who think the ministry or leadership is all about them. It will mean a great deal to those who deeply care about the ministry they are a part of and are seeking to build a ministry that will last. Great leaders and teams are not only concerned about today but are also building in a way that the ministry will remain healthy tomorrow.

By God's grace (and the intercession of our prayer team) I survived my close brush with death and came back to work with an even greater commitment to ensuring that the team I lead is deep and healthy—and to helping other ministries do the same. I realized in a new way how much team matters. Thus, I leave you with these final questions:

- Leaders, if you were taken out of the picture tomorrow, what would happen with your responsibilities and the direction you have set for your team?

- Team members and leaders, is there someone who knows your responsibilities so intimately that he or she could carry your weight if you were suddenly gone?
- Are you intentionally building for the future health of your ministry rather than building for today?

If you would like to interact on any of the concepts in this book or share some of your own experience in working with teams, please write me at tj@addingtonconsulting.com. Comments, criticisms, and suggestions are welcomed and appreciated.

NOTES

How to Read and Use This Book

1. T. J. Addington, *High-Impact Church Boards* (Colorado Springs, CO: NavPress, 2010).

Chapter 1: Fallacies and Practices of High-Impact Teams

1. Tom Rath, *StrengthsFinder 2.0: A New and Updated Edition of the Online Test from Gallup's Now, Discover Your Strengths* (New York: Gallup Press, 2007).
2. Two excellent articles on Emotional Intelligence are Daniel Goleman's "Leadership That Gets Results," *Harvard Business Review*, March–April 2000, reprint number R00204; and Daniel Goleman's "What Makes a Leader," *Harvard Business Review*, January 2004, reprint number R0401H.

Chapter 3: Defining Your Culture

1. Exceptions to this concept are places where pioneer church planting is necessary because there are no believers or instances where missionaries are intentionally planting catalytic church plants to raise up church planters, who are then sent out to plant churches themselves.

Chapter 5: Healthy Team Leaders

1. For more information on strategic initiatives, see chapter 9 of *High-Impact Church Boards*.

Chapter 9: Dangerous Transitions

1. For an excellent discussion on leadership pipelines, see Ram Charan, Stephen Drotter, and James Noel, *The Leadership Pipeline: How to Build the Leadership-Powered Company* (San Francisco: Jossey-Bass, 2001).

ABOUT THE AUTHOR

T. J. ADDINGTON is a senior vice president of the Evangelical Free Church of America (EFCA), an organizational consultant, speaker, and author. He resides in Minnesota with his wife of thirty-three years and is the father of two children, Jon and Steven (Chip). In his spare time he enjoys reading, traveling, writing, and fly-fishing. He is the author of two other books, *High-Impact Church Boards* and *Live Like You Mean It*. T. J.'s passion is to see God's people be all that they can be. Read more from T. J. on leadership issues at www.leadingfromthesandbox.blogspot .com.

More great titles from NavPress!

High-Impact Church Boards

T. J. Addington

978-1-60006-674-0

Discover how to grow strong, intentional, and authoritative church leaders among a world lacking godly leadership.

Live Like You Mean It

T. J. Addington

978-1-60006-673-3

Author T. J. Addington helps you think deeply about the most important issues of life, clarify their purpose, live intentionally, learn to play to their strengths, and make the most of the rest of your life.

Discovering the Bible

Gordon L. Addington

978-1-61521-269-9

Take a journey through the Bible in one year. In *Discovering the Bible*, Gordon Addington, gives you insightful notes and the historical background for each day's reading. See how God unfolds His amazing plan of redemption throughout the entire Bible. Leader's guide included on CD.

To order copies, call NavPress at 1-800-366-7788 or
log on to www.navpress.com.